MAKING SENSE OF 'SHOW, DON'T TELL'

TRANSFORM YOUR FICTION: 3

Copyright © 2021 Louise Harnby

The right of Louise Harnby to be identified as the author of this work has been asserted by her in accordance with the Copyright, Designs and Patents Act 1988. All rights reserved. This book is sold subject to the condition that it shall not, by way of trade or otherwise, be lent, re-sold, hired out or otherwise circulated in any form of binding or cover other than that in which it is published and without a similar condition including this condition being imposed on the subsequent purchaser.

ISBN: 9798715255136

CONTENTS

1. What is shown and told prose?	1
2. The difference between action and intention to act	5
3. Filter words: When the focus is on doing being done	10
4. Body parts doing what's expected	18
5. Expletives – not the sweary kind!	22
6. The art of writing pain and pleasure	27
7. Writing the sound of noise	32
8. What's the weather like?	36
9. Instantaneity without loss of immediacy	40
10. Character description that makes an impression	44
11. The order in which stuff gets done	50
12. Emotionally evocative scenes	55
13. Reading between the lines: Is the telling showing us something?	59
14. The non-viewpoint character's world	64
15. In and around dialogue	68
16. A box of showing tools	76
Glossary	84
Cited sources	87

1. What is shown and told prose?

Why understanding showing and telling is key to craft

Whether you're a fiction writer or a fiction editor, putting in the work to really get your head around how shown and told prose affect story is worth your time, I promise. The knowledge will enable you to revise stylistically with purpose and confidence. Each amendment will be made with care and founded on theory – theory that respects voice, mood, rhythm, and preference.

Showing and telling in a nutshell

Shown prose is usually defined as story and character experience that's related through actions and sensory information. Told prose relies upon exposition. This (likely apocryphal) quote from Chekhov is often cited to explain the principle:

> Don't tell me the moon is shining; show me the glint of light on broken glass.

That's a good summary. However, the canny author and editor will tread with caution; to do otherwise risks hyper-amending at best, butchering at worst. And so to make prose pop we need to heed the following:

- Telling is more than a lack of sensory detail. For while it might shout its presence in some passages, more often than not it's almost hidden in the nuances of just a word or two.
- And, yes, there are occasions when only shown prose will do.
- But there are also occasions when the reader needs only to know that the moon is shining; glints on broken glass are a distraction.
- And there are yet other occasions when the line between told and shown prose is blurry because even told prose can be rich and emotive owing to other stylistic choices, such as tense, narration style and viewpoint.

The decision about whether to show or tell needs to be nuanced. It's true that too much telling can result in a flat, mundane narrative, while showing can add emotional texture that brings a written scene alive and draws the reader deeper into the story. Then again, too much showing can result in overblown, interruptive writing. Strong writing weaves the two together.

We might think of showing as a way of making readers do the work – giving them enough information so that they can imagine how they would feel if what's been revealed on the page were to happen in real life. The deeper the connection, the more immersive the reader experience. That's what the Chekhov quote is alluding to and it's why it's worth understanding the different types of told prose so that we can decide – in the context of the scene – whether and to what degree we should tell or show.

Context is key, however. Once we understand all the ways in which our readers can be told, it becomes clear that abolishing telling from writing would be catastrophic. That's because told prose can be textured too, especially when a novel's written in the first person; it's as if the narrator is having a private conversation with us, or has written us a personal letter. And so the narrative distance is already so short that shown prose might seem absurdly contrived and verbose.

A real-world example

Let's move away from creative writing for a moment and use a real-world example as reference. A care home advertises the following job:

> CARE TEAM LEADER: This would be the perfect role for a registered nurse with team-supervision experience who is ready for lead responsibility. You must have experience in general, dementia and mental-health nursing care. Your respect for older people is equally important. You will show warmth, compassion and support to our residents and their families, helping to promote independence and dignity, and positively enhancing the lives of individuals in our care.

You submit your résumé and cover letter, and are invited for an interview. The day arrives and you come to the care home expecting to be questioned by a panel of staff members about your experience and fitness for purpose. Instead, you're directed to the garden, where the residents are having a tea party.

A few smile at you. One man seems distressed and starts to cry. A woman sits in a chair, licking her lips. There's a beaker of water on a nearby table, but it's out of her reach. You walk over to the woman, move the beaker nearer and ask her if she'd like a drink of water. Then you head for the man, sit near him and ask him if you can help.

The résumé and cover letter are examples of *telling*. They're useful, expository documents through which you explain that you're skilled and compassionate. It's in the garden that you get to *show* it.

Think of the staff looking on as your readers, and of the crying man and the thirsty woman as characters in your book. In a nutshell, told prose explains how things are; shown prose displays it.

Viewpoint considerations

Viewpoint – whose perspective readers view the world of the novel through – is critical to decisions about whether to show or tell in prose because it determines how readers are able to access various characters' emotions. If in the care-home example above you're the viewpoint character, you could *tell* us about an emotion you're experiencing – for example, that you're nervous about the interview. However, that would mean we don't have access to the thirsty woman's internal experience. Instead you'll need to *show* it via what can be observed – perhaps by her licking her lips.

Narrative distance

Writers also need to consider how deeply they want their readers to be immersed in character experience. Think back to the staff watching on in the garden. They're like readers.

If you walk up to the thirsty woman, turn around and call over to the staff, 'I'm just about to do something compassionate,' and then move the beaker nearer to the woman, you force them to focus on what you're *saying to them* and away from the interaction between you and the thirsty woman. In other words, your telling (the explanation) draws them out of the moment (the experience) of compassion. It diminishes the emotional connectedness between them and the scene unfolding before them. When that happens in a novel, the narrative distance expands and the prose can be less immersive.

A layered perspective

Writing and editing are rarely straightforward exercises. The key to careful editing comes in being able to recognize *what* is really being told and whether, despite the surface exposition, something else is being shown in the space between the sentences running across the page.

For that reason, I've included examples of effective told prose throughout this guide. Some illustrate how telling can make for a leaner story. Others remind us that narrators have a voice and a personality; exposition can deepen both. Yet others ensure the reader's gaze is focused where the author intends.

This guide's structure

Each chapter explores different ways in which prose can be shown or told. I start by offering some clue words and phrases to watch out for – indicators that telling is in play. These aren't the root of all evil, examples of what must be obliterated. They're pointers that ask us to consider their purpose and relevance. An overview of what to consider follows. Then we move to examples of shown and told prose, an evaluation of how effective they are, and the tools available to fix any problems.

By pulling apart 'Show, don't tell' and looking at it microscopically, even inexperienced authors and editors will be able to make sense of the concept, and craft solutions where required.

At the end of the guide there's a toolbox with which to develop your showing craft. That's followed by a glossary of key words and phrases – the terminology of fiction writing.

Why there's no place for 'don't'

Fiction writing and revision are subjective. Writers and editors who go searching for clues to told prose but then use a sledgehammer to eradicate every instance will harm the novel.

Effective editing requires an open mind; there's no place for 'don't' in relation to either showing or telling. Instead, there are choices to be made as to how to create a story worth reading, one that's served by the line craft within.

2. The difference between action and intention to act

Clues to potential problems
Here's what to watch out for: *to* [verb], *in an attempt to* [verb], *in order to* [verb], *so as to* [verb].

Overview
Infinitive verb forms are the issue here, in particular the word *to*. For example, *Jeremiah reached forward to shake Margaret's hand*. Infinitives tell readers *why* the characters did what they did, rather than showing *what* they did. Grammatically, they're perfectly acceptable, and some might think me pedantic for addressing them. However, compelling writing is immersive. Action is beloved by writers precisely because the showing of it pulls readers along with a character, and makes them feel part of the experience, as if they're right there in the thick of it.

Even the smallest snags like a misplaced infinitive can widen the narrative distance between reader and character and make the scene less immersive. And given that the fix is so easy, I think it's an issue worth paying attention to.

What to consider

- Are you trying to report action or impending action? They're not the same thing.

- Who is the viewpoint character? If the desire *is* to show intention to act rather than action itself, do readers have access to that motivation? With a viewpoint character, the answer will be yes. With a non-viewpoint character, readers will be restricted to what can be inferred from audible and observable behaviour, not internal motivation.

Problematic told prose: Logic
When the aim of the prose is to report action, the use of an infinitive is problematic because *to* tells us about impending action. We're *told why* a character does something rather than *shown* how or even that they do act.

That's because readers are held in a moment of implausible immobility, one in which we're supposed to believe they're moving but aren't given semantic tools that allow for it.

In the four examples below, the characters never set the drone among the gravestones; the light doesn't get switched on; Carla doesn't receive a phone call, even though she miraculously answers; and I somehow peek through the window even though walking to the car is nothing more than a goal. All the action is impending.

> They parked up by the graveyard next to the busted-up old church **to** set the Holy Stone among the holy stones.
>
> Jan reached up **to** switch on the light. The attic was empty. Almost.
>
> Andrew picked up the phone **in order to** call Carla. She answered on the third ring.
>
> I get out of the car **to** walk towards the caravan. The curtains are open so I peek through the plastic window. No one's home.

Look at what happens when we remove the *to*, introduce a conjunction and tweak the conjugation.

> They parked up by the graveyard next to the busted-up old church **and** set the Holy Stone among the holy stones.
>
> Jan reached up **and** switched on the light. The attic was empty. Almost.
>
> Andrew picked up the phone **and** called Carla. She answered on the third ring.

A conjunction is often a quick and beautiful fix that focuses readers on what the author intended; impending action has become action in the now; and the narrative distance has been reduced. Now we're right there with the characters as the scenes play out.

Jan acts and we go with her. We're shown her intention through that action, and feel closer to her because of it, as if we are her. In the unedited example, she discovered the empty attic and yet the light never got switched on – all we had was her intention to do it. The *and* fixes that problem. And Carla can now answer on the third ring because Andrew actually made a call.

Conjunctions aren't the only option. There are other ways of fixing told motivation-based prose where action is what the author really wants to convey. Let's revisit the caravan example. Each of the following recasts has a slightly different mood, but the *to* has been ditched.

> I get out of the car and walk over to the caravan. The curtains are open so I peek through the plastic window. No one's home.

> I get out of the car, walk over to the caravan, peek through the plastic window. The curtains are open. No one's home.

> I get out of the car. Walk over to the caravan. The curtains are open so I peek through the plastic window. No one's home.

In each case, readers are focused on my journey to the caravan, not the reason why I get out of the car. And now that I'm doing walking rather than just car-exiting, I can get to that caravan and peek through the window.

Problematic told prose: Viewpoint

Infinitives can also interfere with point of view. In this case, it's not immediacy at stake but that we're being told what it's impossible for the viewpoint character to know. Here are a couple of examples:

> I jump over the wall and land on the soft verge. Dan's German shepherd greets me. The dog bares its teeth, preparing **to** bite.

> Matty. The guy was a pain, had done nothing but hold her back all day. Denise shoved him hard in the back. He grabbed the side of the boat **to** steady himself.

In the example with the German shepherd, I'm the viewpoint character. All is well until I meet the dog. It bares its teeth. We're still good. But then the infinitive slips in, and with it I'm now privy to the dog's intention – to bite. It's a step too far. Perhaps the dog's been trained to snarl. Maybe it's more a warning than an impending attack.

The scene could demand I get bitten or escape intact. Either way, what matters is that we're not in the dog's head so we can't be told of its intention. Instead, we must be shown how it behaves, and then what happens.

In the example on the boat, Denise is the viewpoint character. We have access to her thoughts via the free indirect discourse: 'The guy was a pain ...'. That Matty grabbed the side of the boat is fine. In fact, it's a solid example of shown prose because although we don't have access to his intentions or motivations (because we're not in his head) we can make a good guess at what they are from his observable behaviour – grabbing the side of the boat.

However, the infinitive tells us *why* too. That's redundant because we already worked it out, but it's also a viewpoint drop. We can't know; we're not in his head. All we can do is see through Denise's eyes. Yes, it's likely that he's steadying himself, but why not let the reader do the work? His actions are enough to show his motivation.

The fix

Let's fix the viewpoint drop and show action rather than telling of intention we shouldn't be able to access. In the example with the German shepherd, two recasts show what happens, rather than telling what might.

> The dog bares its teeth, leaps forward and clamps its jaw around my arm, puncturing the skin.

> I jump over the wall and land on the soft verge. Dan's German shepherd greets me. The dog bares its teeth and I freeze. It backs off, so I give it a wide berth and trot down the road.

And here are a couple of options for the boat scene.

> Matty. The guy was a pain, had done nothing but hold her back all day. Denise shoved him hard in the back and he grabbed the side of the boat.

> Matty. The guy was a pain, had done nothing but hold her back all day. Denise shoved him hard in the back. He grabbed the side of the boat.

Shown prose that works

Notice how in this example from *Dark Matter* (p. 310), we're told that the non-viewpoint character raises a weapon, but not *why*. Instead, the action stands on its own and the author focuses on what the viewpoint character (Jason) does: gets away fast. We're shown that Jason *believes* the man intends to shoot, but not what the man's actual intention is.

> He raises a gun, and I'm suddenly running in the opposite direction, sprinting down the hallway toward the door at the far end that I'm praying isn't locked.

Told prose that works

There are times when intention *is* the intention. The infinitive form of a verb is a good choice because the author doesn't want to show action, but rather wishes to tell readers about a character's intention, purpose or desire.

Here are some examples. The first is an excerpt from Nuala Ellwood's *Day of the Accident* (p. 94). The others I've made up.

> Her eyes flash with hatred. I go **to** speak, **to** defend myself, but no words will come. Instead I let Sonia guide me away, Barbara's venom ringing in my ears.
> I take deep breaths **to** calm myself.
>
> He'd worked his backside off with this parole officer **to** stay out of trouble.
>
> Arthur went **to** pull Excalibur from the stone but Merlin's scream stopped him in his tracks.
>
> I've made a decision. I'll fill up her petrol tank with diesel **to** trash the engine. That'll teach her.

In all the examples, motivation is the order of the day. We're supposed to focus on the intention – the characters do X for the purpose of achieving Y – and so the infinitives are effective. The action itself is impending, just as it should be.

Summing up

Consider what infinitives are doing to the prose before editing them out. If the characters are meant to be in action, show those actions in the prose rather than telling readers about intention. Replace the infinitives with a conjunction and modify how the verb's conjugated. Or, for a more staccato feel, try commas, or closing the sentence with a full point and starting a new one. However, when it's motivation you want, a *to* plus a verb has the right to stand.

3. Filter words: When the focus is on doing being done

Clues to potential problems
Here's what to watch out for: *noticed, seemed, spotted, saw, realized, felt, thought, wondered, believed, knew, decided, looked at, found him/herself.*

Overview
Every novel includes characters doing and experiencing things. That action needs to be offered in such a way that the reader feels as if they're experiencing it right alongside the narrator. Unless the book is written in an omniscient narration style, we see, hear, smell, touch, feel, think and know what the viewpoint character sees, hears, smells, touches, feels, thinks and knows.

There's a risk that when we're told that this doing is being done, we feel less connected with the viewpoint character. In other words, narrative distance widens. This telling occurs in the form of verbs that remind us that we're outside of the story. They're called filter words.

Filter words remind us that what we're reading is being *told* by someone rather than experienced, or shown, through the eyes of the character. We can think of them as written nudges that denote how a character *comes by* experience rather than *what* they experience.

I see more extensive filtering in books written by less experienced novelists who've not yet learned to trust their characters' voices, who are uncomfortable about playing with devices such as free indirect style, or who are still learning the craft of injecting drama into narrative.

What to consider

- Recognize the role of the viewpoint character. If we're meant to be in their head, are filter words dragging us out?

- Where is the reader's attention? On the viewpoint character's doing or on the object of their actions? If the former, and that's not where the attention should be, it's a told misfire. If it's the latter, that told prose will be justified; it might even be critical to suspense building.

- Would a recast version without filter words declutter the prose or would it remove critical information?
- What's the impact on pace and mood? Too much filtering can add layers of telling that slows down a narrative. However, a well-placed filter word can introduce a more enquiring or deliberative feel to prose.
- Think about the narration style. If it's third person, telling might be a distraction. If it's first person, the filtering could deepen character voice.
- And banning all filter words is a no-no. There will be times when the exposition is required to make sense of the scene.

Problematic told prose: Cluttering that widens narrative distance

Filter words are problematic when they're used too often. They're an indication that a novelist doesn't trust their reader to enter the viewpoint character's head. A pity, because readers do this naturally. Filter words – particularly when they're used as a narrative staple – tap the reader on the shoulder and say, 'You're not in this book. Someone else is experiencing this.' The consequence is a less immediate narrative and flatter character voices.

The following example of exposition is just one of many in the novel it's taken from. In the first, the viewpoint character, Aurora, is a young teenager with a group of older kids she's already uncomfortable around. Then this happens.

> It was a small space. There was just enough room for her to sit, or to kneel. Ahead of her, there was something that gleamed in the dimness. She squinted at it, held out a hand and ran it over the wall of dull silver. She realized that these were piles and piles of carefully folded foil packets held in dozens of clear plastic bags.
> She **didn't need to know** what was in them. Drugs of some kind, she **thought**. Nothing she wanted to know about. (*She Lies in Wait*, pp. 26–7)

The filtering in this excerpt adds extra words that strip the prose of its atmosphere. The author's gone to some trouble to set up a suspenseful scene so that we're wondering what's in that small, dark space. And then, when the big reveal comes, it's not the plastic bags full of drugs that we're shown. It's Aurora's *realizing*. And with that realization, one that can only be hers because we're in her head, is the stark reminder that we're not living that character's experience. It doesn't stop there either; we're told about Aurora's thought, then her guess too.

It's not a case of the odd filter word. The entire book is littered with filtering that widens narrative distance to the point of dislocation, and distracts from what should be a compelling mystery.

The fix

By removing the filter words (and a few other bits of told prose that are addressed elsewhere in this guide), we are offered a suspenseful narrative that comes right from Aurora's head. The prose is leaner, and our attention is now on the cramped dark space and the drugs. We still know it's Aurora seeing, thinking, guessing – it could be no one else because she's the viewpoint character – but the tension is back, the reveal satisfying.

> It was a small space, just enough room for her to sit or kneel in. Ahead, something gleamed in the dimness. She squinted at it, held out a hand and ran it over the wall of dull silver. Piles and piles of carefully folded foil packets held in dozens of clear plastic bags.
>
> Drugs of some kind. Nothing she wanted to know about.

Problematic told prose: Self-awareness

Filter words – particularly when they're used as a narrative staple – tell of an awkward and inauthentic self-awareness about the *how* rather than the *what* of experience.

In the following example, Petra is the viewpoint character. We're in her head and therefore experience events moment by moment as she does. Or we would do if the filter words didn't interrupt, widening the narrative distance between us and her, reminding us that, actually, we're not her. Through them, we're told *how she comes by* the sensory information of the gravel and the aftershave and the knowledge of Phil's proximity.

> Petra scuttled towards the garage and hid behind a large oak tree. She **heard** the sound of Phil's boots on the gravel underfoot and **smelled** the sharp aroma of his awful

aftershave. She **could see** he was close, about two feet away from her.

The telling focuses us on her acts of her hearing, smelling and seeing when it could be showing us the outcome of her using her ears, nose and eyes. Think about when you feel, know or notice something. Are you focused on the actual doing? It's more likely that you're focused on something sensory, like your mood or physical state, or on the object of your attention. And that's usually where the reader needs to be if the narrative is immersive.

The fix

In the recast below, I've removed the filter words so that instead of being told about Petra's acts of her hearing, smelling and seeing, we are shown what happens as a result of her using her senses.

> Petra scuttled towards the garage and hid behind a large oak. Gravel crunched. Rank aftershave tickled her nose. Phil was close now, a couple of feet at most.

Problematic told prose: Viewpoint snags

Narrative viewpoint is critical when it comes to filter words. If your narration style is first, second or third person, each chapter or section will feature a viewpoint character – the person from whose perspective we experience the scene. We're already in their head, so being told that they saw something is redundant if they're reporting visual information.

Ask yourself where you want your reader to focus – on your characters' senses, or what those senses experience? Should readers be watching Petra's doing the seeing, or should they be seeing what Petra sees?

The problem is more profound when authors introduce filter words that tell of a non-viewpoint character's experience-acquisition. That's a viewpoint drop. Here's a tweaked version of the Petra example. She's still the viewpoint character.

> Petra scuttled towards the garage and hid behind a large oak tree. She **heard** the sound of Phil's boots on the gravel underfoot and peeked around the trunk. Phil **noticed** the sweetness of her perfume and turned towards the tree.

Phil's noticing the viewpoint character's scent jars for two reasons. First, it's an explanation that tells us about his noticing, not a display that shows us *what* he's experiencing. But more important, the act of noticing is an internal experience, one we shouldn't have access to because we're not in his head; we're in Petra's.

The fix

Here's a solution that sorts out the filtering and the head-hopping.

> Petra scuttled towards the garage and hid behind a large oak. Gravel crunched and she peeked around the trunk. Phil sniffed the air and turned towards the tree. Damn. Had her perfume given her away?

Now we're shown what Phil does – the actions he takes that Petra can observe from her hiding place. I've used free indirect speech to introduce the question around the perfume so that the experience of its aroma is firmly rooted in her head, not Phil's. Instead, his action – sniffing – shows us that he might have noticed it.

Shown prose that works

Take a look at these three examples of shown prose from published fiction.

> When the dark mellowed, he shuffled inside and sank onto the seat that a long-dead troglodyte had hewn into the cave wall. The familiar coldness seeped through his trousers and into his flesh. (*The Devil's Dice*, p. 1)

> The address is typed on a sticker, the postmark a smudge of ink in the top right-hand corner. (*Let Me Lie*, p. 15)

Notice how they allow the reader to experience viewpoint character experience rather than punctuating it with information about *how* they came by that experience via tells of feeling and seeing. It's a far more immersive experience.

Told prose that works

Filter words, used purposefully, can enrich a novel because the reader benefits from having that sense of the doing being done.

In this first example, Barry is our viewpoint character and he's snooping around an unfamiliar building he has no right to be in.

> He **sees** an elevator, and beside it, a door presumably leading to a stairwell.

> The light above the elevator illuminates.
> A bell dings.
> Barry ducks behind a Lincoln MKX and **watches** through the tinted glass of the front passenger window as the elevator doors part.
> Empty.
> What the hell is this? (*Recursion*, p. 69)

We're initially told that Barry *sees* an elevator, then that he *watches*. Both are filter words but they're perfectly placed because the author wants us to focus on Barry's visual experience – that's what this section of the scene is about. That he sees the elevator is a signal that he's only just noticed it in that moment. In this case, his immediate observation is central to the narrative. The watching that follows is a suspense builder in which our gaze is on Barry as he sneaks a peek and waits to discover who will emerge from the elevator.

In this next excerpt, the POV character is a lawyer investigating a tough case that's keeping him busy.

> When the movie is over, I **realize** I haven't called Karen to ask if she can put me in touch with Keith Franklin. (*Play Dead*, p. 111)

Here the author uses the filter word *realize* to tell us that the character's experiencing a sense of dawning awareness. Without the telling, the prose loses its emotionality. The realization is something that bothers the lawyer, and so once more our focus on that acquisition of experience is intentional.

In the example below, the protagonist is hidden in the shadows, spying on the events taking place inside a military hangar.

> Another jeep pulled up outside, and he could **hear** the clenched barking of an officer. New arseholes were being torn. (*Dead Lions*, p. 291)

The exemplifies why one particular filter word – *hearing/heard* – can be treated with more lenience than other sensory filters. As long as it's not overused it rarely jars because it indicates the viewpoint character's attention on unobservable events. That means it can sometimes intensify, rather than dilute, the reader's emotional connection with the character.

Here's another example. The POV character is having a clandestine conversation in which his companion has just revealed shocking information.

> Reeves just keeps staring at me. I **think** about the orange blur that I assumed was a jumpsuit. I **think** about the secure location. I **think** about the need for secrecy. I **think** about the helicopter coming at night under the cover of darkness and silence. (*Don't Let Go*, p. 276)

If the author had decided to eradicate every instance of his protagonist's thinking in this book, we'd have been denied this powerful example of anaphora – repetition that creates rhythm and mood. And while, of course, it can only be the narrator who's doing the thinking, telling us that doesn't feel like redundant filtering that widens narrative distance. Instead, it draws us in deeper and amplifies our understanding of the character, one who is rolling ideas around in his mind, trying to put the pieces together so he can discover whodunnit.

Finally, in the excerpt below the viewpoint character, Ralph – a police officer – is trying to navigate a large, frenzied mob.

> He **saw** Howie leading Marcy toward the steps, their heads bent as if they were moving into a stiff wind, and **saw** a woman lean forward to give her the finger. He **saw** a man with a canvas newspaper sack over his shoulder and a watch cap crammed down on his head in spite of the heat of the day. He **saw** the portly bailiff shoved from behind and only saved from a nasty tumble when a broad-shouldered black woman grabbed him by the belt. He **saw** a teenage boy with his girlfriend perched on his shoulders. [...] He **saw** waving signs. He **saw** open, shouting mouths, all white teeth and red satin lining. He **heard** someone blowing a bicycle horn: *hooga-hooga-hooga*. (*The Outsider*, p. 155)

This is one paragraph from a whole page of filtering. And yet it is the multiple mentions of what in the main Ralph *saw* that give a richly textured substance to the chaos surrounding him, and the other actors involved in it. Certainly, we are told of doing being done, but that telling has a deeper layer – it shows us a frenzied scanning of the mayhem, and that the police have lost control of the huge crowd.

Summing up

Watch out for filter words that tell readers how characters come by experience rather than showing what's being experienced. Then consider whether a gentle removal will improve the prose. If the prose feels more dramatic and immersive, you've done your novel and your readers a favour.

If, however, you lose something in the revision – like voice, mood, intention, or atmosphere – reintroduce the filters at the appropriate points. Perhaps the reader is meant to focus on the seeing and hearing, and that experience of doing is what will draw them deeper into the viewpoint character's interior space.

4. Body parts doing what's expected

Clues to potential problems
Here's what to watch out for: *with his/her/their* [body part], *shrugged his/her/their shoulders*, *stood to his/her/their feet*.

Overview
Characters' bodies move in multiple ways. They walk, run, move, swim, glide, and tiptoe from A to B such that readers understand their journey. But just as important are their gestures and tics, small movements that can bring them alive and help us visualize not only their actions but also their thoughts and feelings.

Where less experienced authors sometimes come unstuck is by telling readers information that's already been shown adequately through a strong verb.

Furthermore, some movements can only be done with particular body parts. Effective prose *shows* us the action without *telling* us obvious additional information that would be cluttering. Unless the character has a specific physiological difference, they hear with their ears, see with their eyes, stamp and kick with their feet, kiss with their lips, and nod with their heads.

Readers often don't need to know which body part is involved; they can work it out. Additional information might be better focused on the impact of the action rather that the limb or organ that carried it out.

What to consider

- How does the character's body work? Are they differently abled? A person with no arms might use their toes to grasp objects. Are they other than human? Your alien might use its limbs in unfamiliar ways. Setting the scene with one telling nudge might be necessary if the reader is to understand what later verbs are showing.
- Does the body part add necessary information without which the reader can't make full sense of the prose?
- Is the prose cleaner and leaner with or without the body part? Superfluous body parts can end up taking centre stage, and too

often such that their mentions are repetitive. Eye work and smiling mouths are common over-mentions.

Problematic told prose

Here are three examples of body parts telling what we've already been shown. The first three are from drafts of real novels in progress whose authors kindly gave me permission to use them as teaching examples. The fourth is something I made up but come across often.

> A tall, athletic man was sprinting towards him, **his hands** clasping a gun. Kabeya turned right into Long Lane and ran.
>
> Parsons shrugged **his shoulders** and said, 'I can understand that. Nothing is risk-free.'
>
> Kay stands **to her feet** and pushes her sleeves up **her arms**.
>
> His **eyes** glanced at her briefly. Then he turned away.

The first three excerpts are taken from thrillers. There are no aliens or unfamiliar world-building rules, and none of the characters are differently abled. The body parts are therefore superfluous and clutter the prose. Clasping is, by definition, an action done with hands; shrugging is done with shoulders; sleeves are worn by arms; standing implies getting to one's feet.

As for my fourth example, only eyes can do glancing, never mind that a glance is by definition a brief look.

The fix

Here's how those told examples can be fixed without damaging the prose. The revised versions are leaner but the sense is intact. Now we can focus on the action without being bogged down by what body parts are responsible for it.

> A tall, athletic man was sprinting towards him, clasping a gun. Kabeya turned right into Long Lane and ran.
>
> Parsons shrugged. 'I can understand that. Nothing's risk-free.'
>
> Kay stands and pushes her sleeves up.
>
> He glanced at her and turned away.

Shown prose that works

In the following examples, the body parts are absent.

> At the entrance to the same park, Roderick Ho gripped the railings and prayed for something. (*Dead Lions*, p. 286)

> As they approached a checkpoint at the ring road and the inner city, an American MP waved for them to stop. (*To Kill a Devil*, p. 217)

> They scaled a pile of rubble and exited the building, Mason sprinted across the sidewalk at a diagonal trajectory to intercept the speeding jeep. He leapt over a barbed-wired barrier set up by the Russians. Right behind him, Kraus miscalculated and cried out as he stumbled. (*To Kill a Devil*, p. 217)

The verbs in these examples are strong – *gripped*, *waved*, *sprinted*, *scaled*, *leapt*, *stumbled*. Readers are in no doubt about when hands and legs are in play.

Below is an excerpt from *Empire of the Sun* (p. 299) by J.G. Ballard. Notice how the mouth doing the cigarette-sucking is assumed. The eyes doing the gazing are absent. And the hand holding the rolled magazine never makes an entrance, which is as it should be since we're given no reason to think he picked it up with anything but his hand.

> 'Yes ... you must have seen it.' Lieutenant Price fastened the bandages around his bleeding fists. He sucked fiercely on his cigarette. Gazing hungrily at Jim, he picked up the copy of *Life* and left the commandant's office. As the Mustang's engine faded across the paddy fields they could hear Price striding up and down the cell-yard, striking the doors of the cells with the rolled magazine.

Told prose that works

In these four examples, body parts are included.

> The soldier was just a boy – they were both boys. The gun trembled **in his hands**. River plucked it free. (*Dead Lions*, p. 286)

She raised **an eyebrow**. Cracks had appeared in her make-up. 'If it's quiet you want, I can find you a corner.' (*Dead Lions*, p. 287)

The blond rapped **his knuckles** on my window and motioned for me to roll down the glass. (*Ghostman*, p. 169)

[...] but Howie shook **his head**, motioned him back and pointed to the rear door on the curb side instead. (*The Outsider*, p. 149)

In these examples, the exposition is relevant. In the first case, it's the first mention of the boy's being armed. Yes, for the gun to tremble he must be holding it; it cannot be holstered. But there's another layer going on here. This isn't just about the gun; it's about showing us the boy's fear. The gun trembles because his hands are shaking, and that's where our focus is supposed to be.

In the second and third excerpts, removal of the body parts would leave the reader with questions: raised what? Rapped what against the window? In the fourth, removing the head could leave the reader mistakenly thinking Howie had trembled, though notice that Stephen King omits the telling of arms/hands doing motioning and pointing.

Summing up

Some movements need to be accompanied by a telling of body parts for sense. Others don't unless a character's body works differently. If arms, legs and eyes are cluttering the prose, introduce strong verbs that nudge the reader in the right direction – towards the action rather than what's doing the action.

5. Expletives – not the sweary kind!

Clues to potential problems

Here's what to watch out for: *there is/was, there are/were, it is/was, they are/were, that is/was, those are/were.*

Overview

Just so we're clear, this chapter isn't about swearing! We're talking instead about a group of words that serve as place holders or fillers in a sentence. They're called grammatical expletives, and they shift the emphasis in a sentence, meaning they have a syntactic function. However, they don't in themselves contribute anything to our understanding of the sentence in the semantic sense. You might also see them called syntactic expletives. Common examples are *there are* and *it is*.

Take a look at the following pair. The first sentence is introduced by an expletive.

- **There was** a car parked outside the house.
- A car was parked outside the house.

When used well, expletives are enrichment tools that allow an author to play with a narrative voice's register and the rhythm of sentences. And so while they have no semantic function, they have a *showing* function – a kind of backdoor to character mood and scene tension.

When prose is overloaded with expletives, it can feel cluttered with filler words that add nothing but ink on the page – more a shopping list than a narrative, one that's being *told* to the reader. At best, they widen the narrative distance between the reader and the POV character; at worst, they flatten a sentence and destroy suspense and tension.

What to consider

- Different beat patterns can make a story more engaging so there's no reason to obliterate them from a novel.
- Expletives do have a role – a syntactic one. If that's not effective, it's an indication that a recast is in order.

- Will recasting the sentence without the expletives tighten it up or damage the flow?
- Are they used so often that they're more a tic than purposeful manipulation of sentence structure for artistic effect?
- Might their inclusion form a critical part of a narrative technique like anaphora, in which case a recast would be destructive?
- Even if the expletive flattens the prose, might this mirror character mood? If so, its syntactic role has been deployed effectively.
- Which viewpoint is in play? If it's omniscient, the wider psychic distance afforded by the odd grammatical expletive might serve the narration well.

Problematic told prose

Too much telling of what there is or was can rip the immediacy from a scene. Expletives that impede sentence navigation encourage skimming. That's a problem – it means the reader isn't engaged and risks missing something.

Worse still, expletives are, by definition, devoid of a semantic role. If they're not performing their rhythmic or emphasis role, what they're telling – *there is/was* – is empty.

Take a look at these examples from *She Lies in Wait* (pp. 26–27, pp. 348, 360).

> It was a small space. There was just enough room for her to sit, or to kneel. Ahead of her, there was something that gleamed in the dimness.
>
> There was suddenly an agonized expression on Coralie's face. 'What do you mean?'
>
> There was a final cracking, splintering sound that must have been a door being kicked in, and then there was a sudden, complete silence.

In the first excerpt, what's supposed to be the shocking discovery by a naive young teen, one that's revealed in a way designed to drive suspense, is flattened by not one but three expletives. We're bogged down in what there was, not what's being discovered.

In the second, the agonized expression loses its wallop because the strongest verb in the sentence is *was*.

In the third, the tension is diluted by two expletives that add filler and interfere with the rhythm. In this case, they're not performing their syntactic role effectively.

The fix

Here are some possible solutions that restore the immediacy and tension by removing the empty expletives and introducing stronger verbs that show the unfolding events.

> It was a small space, just enough room for her to sit or kneel in. Ahead, something gleamed in the dimness.
>
> An agonized expression erupted on Coralie's face. 'What do you mean?'
>
> There was a crack, a splintering – maybe a door being kicked in – then complete silence.

In the first example, the first expletive remains but the rest of the shopping list is gone now that we've played with the punctuation. And the gleaming in the dimness is action that's shown; the reader assumes it's being experienced by the viewpoint character in the small space.

In the second, the empty expletive and the telling of *suddenly* (which is discussed in a separate chapter) are replaced by a stronger verb that shows the woman's face in action.

In the third, the sentence has been tightened up. The first expletive stands because the syntactic function – drawing attention to the sound – is effective. However, the empty, cluttering telling of the second expletive has been removed.

Shown prose that works

In this example from David Rosefelt's *Dog Tags* (p. 15), the sentence is cast without an expletive so that the subject rather than an empty pronoun introduces the sentence. It lends a gritty immediacy that's appropriate to the scene.

> The explosion is deafening, shocking, and somehow disorienting, and at first I can't tell where it is coming from.

And this excerpt from *Cockroaches* (p. 346) Lee Child avoids expletive overload by simply removing the construction from the third sentence, and creating instead a choppier fragment that reads like gritty speech.

> Now it was different. It was dirty and badly maintained. Stained walls, dull floor, dust all over the place.

Told prose that works

Here's a famous piece of prose that uses expletives galore and masterfully. The opening paragraph of Charles Dickens's *A Tale of Two Cities* is a gorgeous experiment in rhythm that sounds like a told narration, and it's meant to. The expletives, treated anaphorically, bring a steady rhythm to the passage that ensures the reader gives equal weight to the contrasting extremes – from best and worst to hope and despair.

The voice is omniscient, and so all those big ideas squeezed into such a tiny space don't sound overblown. The expletives introduce a detached sense of reportage that forces us forward rather than allowing us to dwell on any of the heavens or hells on offer. It's simultaneously mundane and monstrous, and therein lies the magic.

> **It was** the best of times, **it was** the worst of times, **it was** the age of wisdom, **it was** the age of foolishness, **it was** the epoch of belief, **it was** the epoch of incredulity, **it was** the season of Light, **it was** the season of Darkness, **it was** the spring of hope, **it was** the winter of despair [...]

And here's another from *Cooking for Cannibals* (p. 4) by novelist and screenwriter Rich Leder. The syntactic role of the expletive is in play effectively here too, though this has nothing to do with creating a steady beat. Instead, it's a deliberate flattening technique.

Carrie is the viewpoint character. She's somewhere she shouldn't be and is trying to convince herself that she can cover her tracks. The expletive in the final sentence literally flattens the threatening panic, so that the beat of the prose mirrors her emotional intention.

> To steady herself, she focused on her alibi. Technically, she wasn't here. Her car was parked in a lot on the other side of the San Fernando Valley. Witnesses had seen her with a beer in the Foxfire Room in Valley Village. **There was** a bartender who would confirm it.

And here's an example from *Dog Tags* (p. 1) where omission of the expletive would rip the energy from the opening first line of the chapter and interfere with our understanding of which words we're supposed to emphasize.

> "Andy Carpenter, Lawyer to the Dogs."
> **That was** the *USA Today* headline on a piece that ran about me a couple of months ago.

Summing up

Grammatical expletives are a normal part of language and have every right to be in a novel. Overloading can destroy tension and make for a laboured narrative, but a purposeful peppering can amplify character emotion, moderate rhythm, and make space for the introduction of big themes in small spaces without sensory clutter.

6. The art of writing pain and pleasure

Clues to potential problems
Here's what to watch out for: *in/with/of pain/agony/pleasure/ecstasy*.

Overview
Pain and pleasure are difficult to write about despite the fact that most of us know them all too well. Prose can end up repetitive, overwritten and clichéd in either its shown or told form.

Trusting the reader is a good place to start. If a character's elbow is smashed with a hammer, do we really need to be told that it hurt, that they writhed in agony, that they were wracked with pain? It's complicated by the fact that, in real life, extreme sensory experiences can render people voiceless, incapable of articulating their suffering or their bliss. The challenge for the creative writer is to translate that in a way that's authentic but plausible.

What to consider

- Who owns the sensory experience? While shown prose might unlock a non-viewpoint character's internal experience, it might feel overblown and unrealistically self-aware coming from a viewpoint character, especially if the narration is in first person.
- Think about sentence pace. Does the inclusion of the clue words moderate it such that tension is impaired?
- Consider the scene. Is there time to relay sensory details without distracting the reader from the action, or is there space for contemplation that delves deeper into the experience?
- Might showing the consequences of pain and pleasure be a more interesting alternative? If a character's pain is crushing, they might be shown struggling for breath; if it's gnawing, could they bend and hold their belly? Strong verbs that show a character's response to pain can stand in for told pain and pleasure.
- Emotional reactions can be effective shown alternatives. How does a viewpoint character feel when a hammer hits their elbow

or fingers brush over their skin? Frightened, vulnerable, hopeless, humiliated, overwhelmed, dizzy, devoid of reason?
- Telling can be more effective when we know what type of pain or pleasure is in play and how it manifests through shape and movement. For example, a sharp pain that lances, or a dull ache that gnaws can deepen a reader's sensory experience and shorten the narrative distance.
- Is telling the only thing on offer, or is it framed by a more sensory shown narrative that allows the reader to do more of the work? If so, the told prose might earn its place by taking on a set-up role.

Problematic told prose

In the following examples, the sensory experience is told.

> Damian cried out **in pain** as the brick smashed into his face.

> Mina kisses me and I moan **in ecstasy**.

> Her caress was **pleasure beyond imagining**.

> He switches on the drill and holds it over my kneecap, then pushes it in. The **agony is unbearable**.

> I kiss Mina with hungry lips, and she moans **in ecstasy**.

In the first two examples, the crying out and moaning make sense but *in pain* and *in ecstasy* are told redundancies that clutter the prose. Furthermore, the dynamism in the first example – the smashing brick – is impaired by *in pain*, which moderates the pace and flattens the tension.

The third telling is clichéd, as if the author has bailed out on tackling the sensory experience.

The fourth is trickier. It depends on the writer's intention. If they want to avoid dwelling on the torture, this could stand. If, however, the purpose is to give readers insight into the experience, a visceral shown alternative could be more effective.

The last example is a viewpoint drop. I'm the viewpoint character so readers have access to my internal experience. What we don't know is why Mina moans. Hopefully, it's because I'm such a great kisser, but it shouldn't be told. She could be faking it!

The fix

Let's look at how we might edit those examples in a way that shows the pain and pleasure rather than telling them.

> The brick smashed into Damian's face, and he cried out.
>
> Mina kisses me and I moan.
>
> Her caress robbed him of reason and consequence. Wife, home, kids – remembered but insubstantial, like ghosts.
>
> He switches on the drill, holds it over my kneecap, and pushes it in. A white heat explodes in my head and I'm reduced to nothing but a raw scream.
>
> I kiss Mina with hungry lips and she moans, her breath catching.

In the first two examples, I've simply deleted the telling, leaving the strong verbs *cried out* and *moan* to do their job. They show well enough.

In the third, the cliché is replaced by a deeper shown sensory exploration of the viewpoint character's dislocation. The focus is on emotional response. Overworked shown erotica can descend into the absurd if not handled with care. Read Elizabeth Benedict's *The Joy of Writing Sex* to learn how to show and tell sex well.

In the fourth, I've experimented with a more detailed showing of the character's suffering that focuses on the consequences of the pain rather than the pain itself. For more examples of how physical suffering might be shown, download 'Pain: Type, shape, and reaction nudges'.

In the fourth, I've deleted the motivation behind the moan and instead focused on shown audible behaviour from which readers can infer ecstasy.

Shown prose that works

Here are four published examples of prose that avoid the telling of pain and pleasure and instead show us how they manifest through sound, movement, colour and shape.

First up is *The Poppy Factory*, in which William Fairchild uses sound and movement to show pain. There's a detached, contemplative feel to this excerpt that reflects, perhaps, a wish on the character's part not to revisit how the suffering actually felt.

> When you stop screaming and look up, the sky is dark and you can't hear the guns any more, only the sound of someone moaning softly. It takes a few moments before you realise it's yourself.

In *The Poison Artist* by Jonathan Moore (p. 155), the character is drunk on Emmeline, consumed by her. His pleasure is never mentioned; it's shown entirely through his emotional response and what he can touch.

> He was dizzy now. There was the wine, but the real intoxicant was Emmeline. She was inside of him, running through his veins and crossing the barrier to his brain. The slippery silk of her dress, and her bare skin underneath it.

In *Don't Let Go* (p. 280), Harlan Coben has already devoted a short paragraph to told pain, though it's richly described ('the kind of pain that closes down everything else, that makes you recoil to avoid any more of it'). Further down, he *shows* us instead the impact on the body.

> Then with a gleeful smile, he pushes the device—stun baton, electric cattle prod, I don't know—against my torso.
> I start to convulse.
> He does it again. My muscles don't work anymore.

And, finally, look how Milton does it. In this excerpt from *Paradise Lost*, we're left in no doubt as to Satan's physical suffering, and yet there's barely a mention of it. Instead, it is displayed through the effort of his movements ('uneasy steps'), how the fire sought to conquer him ('torrid clime smote on him'), the detail in the environment ('burning marle', 'inflamed sea') that 'he so endured'.

> He walked with, to support uneasy steps
> Over the burning marle, not like those steps
> On Heaven's azure; and the torrid clime
> Smote on him sore besides, vaulted with fire.
> Nathless he so endured, till on the beach
> Of that inflamed sea he stood, and called
> His Legions, Angel forms [...]

Told prose that works

In the following excerpt from *Recursion* (p. 312), the viewpoint character, Barry, and his wife are racing to complete a time-critical task, and hampered catastrophically by radiation burns following a nuclear explosion.

> He powers [the skullcap] on and places it carefully on top of his wife's head, which is blistering over.
> The second-degree burns on his face **are entering the arena of excruciating**. There's morphine in the medical cabinet, calling to him, but there's also no time.
> [...]
> In sharp contrast to her nuclear-sunburned hands Helen's forearms are creamy and smooth, protected from the initial flash by her parka and several layers of shirts and thermal underwear. It takes him several tries with his ruined fingers to thread the IV into her vein.

The author doesn't avoid a brief set-up *telling* of Barry's pain – the bold text. The brevity means the suffering isn't ignored, but neither does it impede the action. And that action is where the author wants readers to focus because that's how the task – their salvation – will be completed. The action is also where the shown suffering (the blistering on Helena's head; the morphine calling; Barry's ruined fingers) occurs, observable manifestations that leave us in no doubt that the characters must be in pain.

And on p. 314, readers are told there's agony, but also its hue (bright), its shape (rod) and how it moves (knifes).

> A bright rod of agony knifes through the back of his skull [...]

Even though it's told, it has substance because of the strong adjectives and verbs in play.

Summing up

Non-viewpoint character pain and pleasure can be shown by audible and observable behaviour. When we're in a viewpoint character's head, we can access the internal experience too. That can be told if showing would be an intrusion that distracts readers from the action, or shown via the environment and emotional response when the detail deepens character and drives the story forward. As always, context is key.

7. Writing the sound of noise

Clues to potential problems
Here's what to watch out for: sounds/sounded, *the sound of*, *the noise of*.

Overview
Told audio information can, if overused, widen the narrative distance between reader and story by focusing attention away from what's being heard and onto the hearing. Phrases such as *sound of* and *noise of* act as filters similar to those discussed in Chapter 3. The result could be a flatter narrative that's overly cluttered.

What to consider

- Might *sound* or *noise* be swapped for richer nouns that better show the type of sound? A bang, a clatter, a thud, a roar, an echo, a rumble and a screech are different in terms of resonance, duration, pitch and tone.

- Is sound being told *and* shown? In that case, there's room to tighten the prose.

- For a richer showing and its impact on character experience, consider weaving in the consequences of sound – emotional (for example, fear) and physical (nauseating).

- Even if the sound can only be told because it's unidentifiable, can interesting adjectives provide information about shape, tone or pitch?

- Does the sound require a telling nudge so as to make sense as auditory experience?

Problematic told prose
Let's look at some examples of told sound and evaluate their impact on the prose.

> **The sound of** engines in the disused aqueduct is deafening. The business of racing is underway.

> She snuggled in the chair, lulled by the **sound of** raindrops against the window.
>
> Ten minutes pass. She doesn't come. Ten more. Maybe she hasn't made it. There's the **sound of** an explosion, and smoke billows from beyond the treeline. A **noise** from behind makes me freeze. The voice that follows it is almost jaunty.
>
> From around the back of the house comes the **noise of** clattering pans.
>
> The **sound of** my phone dings in my pocket. I pull it out and read the text.

The prose feels cluttered with mundane telling that gives the reader little to latch on to. We know there's auditory experience to be had but it's like wearing ear plugs; the texture is missing.

Furthermore, in the fourth example, *noise of* isn't just a tell; it's a double tell. *Clattering* is a sound by definition. And in the fifth, there's a logic flop; it's the phone, not the sound of the phone, that should be doing the dinging.

The fix

Now let's tighten up the narrative with richer shown alternatives that get rid of the clutter and focus the reader on *what* the character's hearing.

> The rumble of engines in the disused aqueduct is deafening. The business of racing is underway.
>
> She snuggled in the chair, lulled by the pitter patter of raindrops against the window.
>
> Ten minutes pass. She doesn't come. Ten more. Maybe she hasn't made it. There's a boom, and smoke billows from beyond the treeline. A rustle from behind makes me freeze. The voice that follows it is almost jaunty.
>
> From around the back of the house comes the clattering of pans.
>
> My phone dings in my pocket. I pull it out and read the text.

In the first three fixes, *sound* and *noise* are replaced with more descriptive nouns (*rumble, pitter patter, boom, rustle*). In the fourth, it's a quick fix

– the double tell has been deleted and the syntax tweaked. And in the fifth, allowing the verb to stand on its own shows the sound and restores logic.

Shown prose that works

In these published excerpts, notice how the authors keep the narrative distance tight by showing sound. The ringing doorbell, the screaming city, the deafening blast and the invasive ringtone are quite sufficient. We don't need to be told that there's *noise* or *sound*.

> I head up to the bedroom now and start to shed my shirt, when the doorbell rings. (*Don't Let Go*, p. 16)

> As the city screams with incoming sirens, Jessica shrieks, "What's happening? What is *happening*?" (*Recursion*, p. 264)

> He hears voices yelling in the stairwell and then a deafening blast that sets his ears ringing—a grenade or a charge. (*Recursion*, p. 297)

> Earlier that morning, she'd groaned at the invasive ringtone from her partner's iPhone. […] How could such a small slab of silicone produce so much noise? (*Insidious Intent*, p. 14)

And in this example from Adrian McKinty, the escalation of sound is shown through not only the rumble and apocalyptic turbines, but also the physical impact on the crockery and furnishings.

> The occasional rumble of riot, gunfire and explosion. Nothing that Carrickfergus's seasoned sleepers couldn't handle. But then the comparative quiet was shattered by the apocalyptic turbines of a CH-47 Chinook. Everything began to rattle. A coffee cup fell off my mantelpiece. A picture came down. (*The Cold Cold Ground*, p. 22)

Told prose that works

In the following example, *sound* works because without it we might momentarily trip, thinking the scratching refers to the physical act of relieving an itch.

> A scratching sound in the eaves makes Ava look up. Her skin crawls. Mice?

The telling ensures we're focused on an auditory rather than physical experience, but the addition of the crawling skin adds emotional texture to her experience of the sound.

Telling sounds can perform a suspense-building function too. In the following example, the quality of the sound is emergent. As the character moves from confusion to understanding, so the sound shifts from being told to shown.

> It's pitch black. He feels along the wall, edges into the corner, and waits. The silence is broken by **a sound** from the end of the hallway that he can't make out. It comes again, now a sibilant whisper than bounces lightly off the walls. Then louder. Not a hiss. A single word. *Missing*.

In the scene below from *No One Home* (p. 382), the viewpoint character has been abducted and bound so that he's unable to see anything but the wall and floor space in front of him. His auditory perception is everything; it's the only sense he can use meaningfully. And that's why the telling of sound works because the author wants us focused on the character's experience of *doing* hearing as well as *what*'s being heard.

> I could hear the same **noises** outside – the city, its hum, the occasional car engine and siren – it was just the carpet and wallpaper that had changed.

Summing up

Sound can be shown or told depending on where the reader's focus needs to be and whether the noise is identifiable. Use strong descriptive nouns that show the type of sound if you can. If telling is required, weave in texture through description that shows the sensory impact of the noise – how the sound makes the character feel.

8. What's the weather like?

Clues to potential problems
Here's what to watch out for: mundane information dumps such as *it was snowing*, *it had started to rain*, *it's hot*.

Overview
The time of day, the time of year and the weather conditions ground actors in their reality and help the reader deepen their immersion in character experience.

Sometimes it's enough to know that a thick blanket of snow is covering the ground because the author's intention is to make that clear and move onto something more interesting.

At other times, prose will be enriched by seeing through the lens of character experience. Does the snow, the darkness, or the fact that it's autumn put obstacles in their way emotionally or physically, or might it liberate them? That's the kind of information that turns a told information dump into an evocative shown reader experience, one that helps them enter the story.

In other words, the weather, the time of day and the seasons can be tools that serve plot and characterization.

What to consider

- How does the weather, time of day or the season affect the characters physically? Does it make them sweat or shiver, or impede their vision, or make their shirt stick to their back?
- How does the weather, time of day or the season affect them emotionally? Do they feel afraid, uncomfortable, exposed, exhausted, frustrated, sad, elated or nostalgic?
- Might a pleasant or chilling memory be evoked?
- Can we access a deeper understanding of character personality or some of their backstory?
- Might the weather mirror/symbolize a character's mood or foreshadow events?

Problematic told prose

Told prose is problematic when it goes nowhere and seems to serve no purpose. The seasons, time of day and weather become nothing more than boring information dumps that sit flat on the page. Here are two examples.

> Autumn had arrived, and it was dark and colder than usual for the time of year. Mario put the down the book and peered out the window.
>
> Thick snow blanketed the drive. Sara parked the Land Rover in the garage and grabbed her phone from the glove compartment. Damn. Still no word from Padraig.

Notice how there's no connection between the character and their environment. In these two examples, it's a lost opportunity to show their experience and place the reader in their heads.

The fix

Here's how we might fix those paragraphs by creating a little entanglement.

> Mario put down the book and rubbed his bare arms, warming them against the autumn chill. Just a hint of frost sparkled on the moonlit windowpane. Unusual this early in the year.
>
> Thick snow blanketed the drive. Sara inched forward, both hands tight on wheel as the Land Rover's back tyres found ice beneath and spun. She made it into the garage and grabbed her phone from the glove compartment. Damn. Still no word from Padraig.

Knowing how Mario and Sara experience the cold, dark autumn night and the snowy drive gives purpose and substance to those environmental entities and the characters acting within them. The autumn chill is now something that's being felt by Mario. And Sara is on edge, waiting for a call. Her interaction with the ice and snow mirrors this.

Shown prose that works

Here's an excerpt from *The Ghost Fields* by Elly Griffiths (p. 135). Her books are typically set in Norfolk, where the wind is a thing! The protagonist and viewpoint character Ruth is in a graveyard along with a TV crew and some of her colleagues. It would have been easy for her to tell us it's windy and leave it at that, but Griffiths goes further and grounds Ruth in her environment by showing us how the wind affects the bouquets surrounding the recently dug grave. The mention of cellophane allows us to see and hear the wind's touch.

> The wind is getting up now. It is riffling through the flowers around the new grave, making the cellophane flap like the wings of a great wounded bird.

And right at the beginning of the book (p. 1), Griffiths opens with a statement about the weather that while written in third person holds the essence of first. Yes, we're told that it's the hottest day of the year but we're also shown how the heat affects Barry – his sweating.

She takes it a step further and uses the temperature as a tool through which to introduce us to how his mind works – what clothes he wears, how often he washes, what manhood means to him, and his disdain for the 'foreign or worse'. The reader is supposed to dislike Barry, and it's through the heat that we are shown this.

> It is the hottest summer for years. A proper heatwave, the papers say. But Barry West doesn't pay much attention to weather forecasts. He wears the same clothes winter and summer, jeans and an England t-shirt. It's sweaty in the cab of the digger, but he doesn't really mind. Being a man is all about sweat; anyone who washes too much is either foreign or worse.

And in *The Cold Cold Ground* (p. 23), Adrian McKinty doesn't tell us it's a cold, wet and windy summer. Instead he uses strong verbs (tugged, pounded, shivered) that show us the impact on a window and his protagonist.

> Wind tugged at the gutters. Rain pounded off the window. I shivered. This was evidently going to be another "year without a summer" for Ulster.

Told prose that works

Telling can work when an author wishes to create a sense of reportage. Perhaps the character is remembering snippets of information. Or maybe giving anything more that the bare facts would distract from the action. In those cases, showing would feel contrived.

And if the weather/season/time of day isn't that important, let the reader use their imagination to fill in the blanks. Just a quick telling is enough.

In the excerpt below, McKinty wants us focusing on 'the incident' that his protagonist is remembering – something that haunts him. He gives us just enough so that we can place the character, but we're not bogged down by showing. That's entirely appropriate because that's not where our character's head is. Maybe the street was confettied with blossom. Maybe the yellow of the daffodils was soothing against the concrete backdrop of the run-down office block. Our character doesn't care to comment because this shopping list of time and place is but a lead-up to 'the incident'.

> And for the second time in twenty-four hours I thought about *the incident*. [...]
> It was 2 May 1974. I was two years into my PhD programme. A nice spring day. I was walking past the Rose and Crown Bar on the Ormeau Road just twenty yards from my college digs. (*The Cold Cold Ground* (p. 23)

Summing up

Pick when to show and when to tell. If the weather/season/time of day is important, and showing its effect on characters or objects would deepen understanding and immersion, go for it.

If a lighter reportage would ensure that the prose is action-centred, higher in tension, or focused on another more important aspect of the story in that moment, an economical tell will be enough to set the scene without swamping it.

9. Instantaneity without loss of immediacy

Clues to potential problems
Here's what to watch out for: *immediately, suddenly, instantly, abruptly, rapidly, unexpectedly, quickly, all of a sudden, in an instant, in a second, the next thing he/she/they knew, before he/she/they knew it.*

Overview
This chapter focuses on now-nudges. They're used with good intention – to convey immediacy – and yet all too often they're unnecessary and clutter a narrative.

Instead, the reader is pulled out of the story, as if the author has tapped them on the shoulder and whispered, 'Hey, something big is coming. Just giving you a heads-up. Now you know, you can carry on reading.'

Then again, now-nudges can be useful indicators of a shift in emotion or pace, one that's short-lived. That momentary experience needs to be told in order for the reader to be able to take that fleeting journey with a character.

What to consider

- Readers are good at sensing nowness. Consider whether you can enhance the pace or enrich the sense of tension without telling them that this is what you're doing.

- Would the prose be richer, clearer and more immersive without a now-nudge or with it? There's no right or wrong answer – every case must be decided on its own merit.

- Are the now-nudges being used to make up for a sentence-pacing problem? If so, a recast that tightens up the prose could eliminate the need for now-nudges.

- Think about fights, realizations, emotional displays, grisly action, unexpected sounds and shock events, and the verbs used to describe character experience. Is the now-nudge *repeating* what's already shown from strong verbs in the prose?

- Is it being used *instead of* a stronger verb that could deliver instantaneity?
- Might a sense of instantaneity be better shown with sentence fragments and asyndeton (the omission of conjunctions to accelerate rhythm)?

Problematic told prose

Let's start with some examples and evaluate why the now-nudges are telling rather than showing.

> Suddenly, the masked man launched himself forward and crashed into Jake.

> Immediately, Ash's face lit up with excitement.

> Instantly, the woman's torso exploded.

> The phone trilled suddenly from his inside pocket.

> In the next instant, Emma slammed on the brakes and the car skidded to a halt.

Take a look at the verbs in those examples – *launched, lit up, exploded, trilled, slammed*. All are imbued with an immediacy, which renders the now-nudging adverbs and adverbials superfluous. Not only are they repetitive, they're also interruptive. The very thing the author wishes to convey – nowness – is anything but because the reader's no longer in the moment with the character; they're one step ahead thanks to the tap on the shoulder.

Tim Weaver is a smashing storyteller and I devour his David Raker mysteries. Still, I think he could have done without the told instantaneity in these two excerpts from *No One Home* (p. 103, p. 222).

> He looked a second time as he got to the apex of the road, where the Black Gale sign stood.
> Then he was gone.
> I immediately broke into a run.

> It was definitely a man.
> He stopped.
> As soon as he did, I instantly sensed something was wrong, the movement so sudden and expected that it had to have been deliberate.

In the first example, *broke* is a dynamic verb that shows us the immediacy. The told *immediately* is redundant. In the second, *as soon as he did* and *instantly* are doing the same thing. The paragraph is laboured and mars the tension.

The fix

The fixes are often one of the least invasive forms of stylistic editing – a simple deletion.

> The masked man launched himself forward and crashed into Jake.
>
> Ash's face lit up with excitement.
>
> The woman's torso exploded.
>
> The phone trilled from his inside pocket.
>
> Emma slammed on the brakes and the car skidded to a halt.
>
> He looked a second time as he got to the apex of the road, where the Black Gale sign stood.
> Then he was gone.
> I broke into a run.

In the second Weaver example, I've gone even further and tightened up the final line, removing all the telling and leaving the action in the now. This scene is a first-person narration, meaning we're right inside the viewpoint character's head. Everything he does, the reader does with him in that moment. Now-nudges pull us out of that space and destroy the tension.

> It was definitely a man.
> He stopped.
> Something was wrong, the movement so sudden and expected that it had to have been deliberate.

Shown prose that works

In the following excerpts from *Orphan X* (p. 340) and *22 Dead Little Bodies* (p. 173), notice how neither author feels the need to nudge the reader into immediacy. They trust us to move through each moment with their characters, showing the nowness with action and strong verbs (for example, *rushed* in the second example), rather than telling it with adverbs.

> He was ten meters away when Candy burst out, her raised fist firing muzzle flares. [...] He scissor-kicked for her Achilles, but she leapt over him, her hand swinging to aim as he popped to his feet. He lunged inside her reach, grabbing the gun as it grazed his cheek. Her hand blocked the rising shotgun.
>
> Colour rushed up Olivia's cheeks. 'Now look what you've gone and done!'

Told prose that works

In the following excerpt from *Recursion* (p. 345), the now-nudge is effective because it shows Slade's shock as seen by the viewpoint character. It tells us that Slade hadn't come to terms with his actions over a period of time; rather the realization had punched him in the face. It's told prose in terms of the time frame, but it shows us something deeper – a distinct emotional shift that happens at pace. Removing *suddenly* means we'd lose this knowledge.

> The look on Slade's face, glowing in the light of distant nuclear fires, was not the look of a lying man, but of one who had **suddenly** come to terms with what he'd done.

In the example below, the inclusion of a now-nudge changes our perspective of Pip's situation. There's a subtle immediacy to his discomfort. It has emerged only now; in the seconds before, he'd watched but not felt threatened. The telling is one of a journey.

> There were ten of them, all big, corralling the guy into the corner. Pip watched, feeling **suddenly** vulnerable.

Summing up

The best way of checking whether now-nudges are necessary is by removing them and reading the sentence out loud. If the tension has dropped, or motivation or mood has become ambiguous, you can either reinstate them or revise the sentence. If you've used them a lot, however, your prose will likely be enriched without them.

10. Character description that makes an impression

Clues to potential problems

Here's what to watch out for: adjectives and adjectival phrases that tell of colour, age, height, weight; lists of the clothes that a character's wearing.

Overview

Knowing what characters looks like helps readers imagine them. Core characters aren't cardboard cutouts. They're people that readers should want to engage with, get to know, love or despise, detest, or invest in. Like people in real life, characters have texture that can be enriched by physical description.

Expository lists of their traits indicate telling that might leave a reader feeling like the author's driven a steamroller over the prose – and the poor character described within it. Alternatives that are shown to us via a character's backstory, mood, comfort levels and interaction with their environment can be superbly immersive.

However, that texture isn't always appropriate. It can get in the way of story and be distracting. And so I'll also offer an example of told physical character description that works because of the way the way it's written and the context within which it's delivered.

What to consider

- Narration style and tense, and how those impact on narrative distance: first person or third-person limited; past or present, for example.
- The length of the description: A detailed shown description could feel overblown, more purple prose than emotional engagement. A detailed told description could make readers want to skim over the information dump. Shown and told prose can both be lean and all the more effective for it.
- How the scene is paced: If dramatic tension's in play, too much shown character description could put the brakes on the action and

flatten the tension, particularly if it's more than a few nudges. In a more contemplative setting, telling might drive it forward.

- What kind of mood the character's in: A shown description of the character's physicality could intensify the reader's understanding of their emotional state. Told prose might flatten it.

- How central the character is to the story: If they're key to the cast, shown prose could deepen our understanding of character arc – their personality, motivations, backstory and how they change. If they make only a fleeting appearance, a shorter told description might be a better choice.

- What the author wants us to discover: Does the choice of shown or told prose help the reader focus on the important information or get in the way of it? Sometimes telling of one thing is a vehicle for the showing of something else.

Problematic told prose

Here's an example of a told physical description of a viewpoint character offered in a third-person limited narrative. It's exposition – information about what John does, how old he is, what he's wearing, and a little about his messy hair.

> Thirty-two-year-old John Mannering pushed through the door of the pathology lab where he worked as an assistant. He wore a white lab coat and a surgical scrubs hat over his unruly blonde hair.

The description of John is flat, like a shopping list. John is a viewpoint character, which means we experience the scene through his eyes, ears and emotions. And yet we feel distant from him, as if watching through a long lens. His experience is dislocated from ours. And the risk is that we don't care about him, even though we should because we're going to see a lot of him.

The fix

Here's how that information could be shown rather than told in a way that textures the characterization.

> John Mannering pushed through the door of the pathology lab and wrinkled his nose. The smell still got to him, even after a decade in forensics. He'd hoped that by

the grand age of thirty-two he'd have gotten over it, but the teenage impostor was tapping on his shoulder yet again. A greasy strand of blonde fringe tickled his right eye; he pushed it under his scrubs hat. His hair wasn't the only thing that needed a wash; so did his lab coat; the white cotton was already stained with coffee.

In the revised version, John's physical description is unveiled through internal experience. There's sensory information available – how the blonde hair is irritating his eye – and we can use this to unveil the hair colour and the scrubs hat. His impostor syndrome is a vehicle through which we discover what else he's wearing, how old he is, and how long he's been doing the job. But we learn something about him too – that he lacks confidence.

It's emotion-based detail, rather than just a list, and that makes it more connective. The narrative distance shortens. Instead of the view through a long lens, we're in the lab with him.

A note on skin colour

Avoid using food-based adjectives to describe skin colour. These can be offensive, and smack of cliché, colonialization, appropriation and fetishizing. Skin colour alone isn't a particularly good indicator of ethnicity anyway, but if it is going to be offered, there are other ways to do it that don't involve food.

There's some excellent guidance on the Writing with Colour blog: 'POC and Food Comparisons' and 'Description Guide – Words for Skin Tone'.

Shown prose that works

Now for a few examples of effective shown character description.

In the first excerpt, Vanessa is the viewpoint character. The authors weave her physical description into a narrative about the challenges she endured when her marriage to a wealthy hedge-fund manager broke down. And so we don't just learn what Vanessa looks like; we also discover that she's traumatized, that she's not been eating well, that she's struggling with money, that she's dealing with a loss.

> I shower, then blow-dry my hair, noticing my roots are visible. I pull a box of Clairol Caramel Brown from under the sink to remind myself to touch them up tonight. Gone are the days when I paid—no, when Richard paid— hundreds of dollars for a cut and color.

> [...]
> I stare at the dresses lined up in the armoire with an almost military precision and select a robin's-egg-colored Chanel. One of the signature buttons is dented, and it hangs more loosely than the last time I wore it, a lifetime ago. I don't need a scale to inform me I've lost too much weight; at five feet six, I have to take in even my size 4s. (*The Wife Between Us*, p. 11)

This is sensory character description that uses reflection, backstory, and the process of change to unveil height, weight, hair colour and shoe size such that readers feel emotionally engaged on two levels: with what they can see in the mirror with Vanessa, and with why she looks as she does.

In the second example below, the character traits are not centre-stage; rather, it's how they *affect* the protagonist that's front and centre – the incongruence of what's observable now contrasted with what might have once been.

> He tried to remember whether the high-pitched, front-of-mouth lisp was new or had always been there. A strange thing in someone in her forties, whose face had laughter lines and furrows under the make-up. (*She Lies in Wait*, p. 137)

And in this final example, the man's muscularity, hair colour, facial hair and bone structure are weaved into an intimate viewpoint-character voice that's laced with experience.

> The standard button-down-with-khakis uniform of a middle-school teacher couldn't hide the fact that he had muscles in places that men in their forties had generally replaced with beer and fried meat. His scraggly beard was more of a five o'clock shadow. The gray at his temples gave him a wizened air of mystery. He had one of those dimples in his chin that you could use to open a bottle. (*The Good Daughter*, p 46)

Her appreciation of his physical traits is shown in the 'beer and fried meat' reference. The grey hair is framed in terms of the sense of mystery he evokes in her. And the free indirect style of 'that you could use to open a bottle' is intimate so that it feels more like she's gossiping with us than relaying expository information.

Told prose that works

In this excerpt, the narrator, who in the past sought counselling, introduces us to a character who will play a secondary role in the story, only popping up now and then.

> I found it – in the form of Ruth, a psychotherapist referred to me through the university counselling service. Ruth was white-haired and plump, and there was something grandmotherly about her. She had a sympathetic smile – a smile I wanted to believe in. (*The Silent Patient*, p. 20)

This told description is a short, sweet list of four observable traits: hair colour, weight, manner and type of smile. What's interesting here is that by telling us just a few things about what she looks like, he *shows* us his own state of mind – 'a smile I wanted to believe in'.

It's those seven words that are loaded with sensory information; that's where the showing is. He's troubled, perhaps even desperate, in need of comfort. Nothing else about Ruth's physicality – how tall she is, what colour her eyes are, how she moves, the pitch of her voice, how old she looks, or what she's wearing – is important, and so the author doesn't waste our time trying to be clever with the unveiling of it. It's a good reminder that sometimes character description should be told, and told quickly so as not to distract from what's important.

Consider narration style too. Here's an excerpt from *The Godmother* (pp. 17–18).

> I'm 53 years old. My hair is long and completely white. It went white very young, as did my father's. For a long time I dyed it because I was embarrassed, then one day I was sick of having to keep an eye on my roots and I shaved my head to let it grow out. Today it seems to be all the rage... Whatever, it goes with my Patience-blue eyes, and clashes less and less with my wrinkles.
>
> My mouth is slightly lopsided when I speak, so that the right-hand side of my face is a bit less wrinkled than the left. It's the result of a subtle hemiplegia caused by my initial crushing. It gives me a certain working-class look, which, together with my strange hairstyle, is not uninteresting. I'm fairly solidly built, carrying five kilos extra – after putting on thirty during each of my two pregnancies when I gave free rein to my passion for large

colourful cakes, fruit jellies and ice creams. At work I wear monochrome suits – grey, black or anthracite – that are unaffectedly elegant.

I take care to be well-groomed so my white hair doesn't make me look like some old beatnik.

Hannelore Cayre's character, Patience, tells us information – about her age, the shape of her mouth, her wrinkles, her weight, her work suits, her well-groomed appearance. The first-person, present tense narration style makes the narrative distance intimate; it's as if Patience is in the room with us. The writing is relaxed, conversational. Shown prose in this context would feel contrived and inauthentic.

It's that artful conversational first-person voice that allows Cayre to make magic from the mundane. Despite the length, the description holds our attention because, yes, it's telling, but it's being done by someone who could be our friend, our mother, our sister, a neighbour. The mood is reflective but chatty. Shown prose would have made the character's conversation with us drag; we might have thought her pompous and verbose. Instead, we can sit back and enjoy the ride because Patience doesn't dilly-dally.

This passage demonstrates how textured told character description can be in the hands of a first-person narrator because Patience's telling is done in a voice that evokes a sense of the woman talking to us: she's stoic, no-nonsense, and there's just a hint that perhaps she wouldn't think twice about giving us the finger if she felt we were judging her. Her journey is evident from the information about how she matured from a younger woman dying her hair to an older one who'd 'got sick of having to keep an eye on my roots' and shaved it off.

And so, like the example from *The Silent Patient*, the author tells the character's physicality, but uses their voice to show something else: personality and change.

Summing up

Exposition can flatten character description *if* that's all that's going on. If the description lacks voice and emotion, consider weaving in texture that considers mood, environment, self-reflection, and contrast. However, when that telling has a function – to allow the reader access to more interesting information about that character's arc or their current state of mind; or because the narrative style and distance are so immediate that showing would make the prose overworked – told prose might well be the order to the day.

11. The order in which stuff gets done

Clues to potential problems
Here's what to watch out for: *before*, *after*, *when*, *during*.

Overview
When writers use words that tell the order of play – explicit chronologies of action – there's a risk that readers will focus on timeline rather than story. That distraction can reduce engagement.

Using the likes of *before*, *after*, *when* and *during* can be indications of authorial insecurity. The writer hasn't learned to trust the power of their words on the page, or the ability of their readers to perceive the meaning behind those words. Some authors also fear that their writing will come across as too 'plain' or 'simple'. Chronological nudges are an attempt to ornament the prose.

What to consider

- Telling readers that X was done before doing Y, or after doing Z, is akin to saying: 'Hey, just in case you're not clever enough, let me spell it out for you.' It's a dumbing-down that readers in the know won't appreciate.

- Consider whether the inclusion of *before* or *after* is necessary. It often isn't. If a character's shuddering occurs at the beginning of a sentence, the reader will assume that shuddering is what's happening right now. If a new action follows that shuddering, the reader will assume that – just like in real life – the moment has passed and something else is happening in the new now of the novel.

- What's the reader focusing on? When writers create immersive fiction, the reader feels as if they are in the moment – this is happening, now that, now the other. *Before* and *after* are distractions that focus the reader on when rather than what's happening. The former is telling; the latter is showing.

- Are these timeline nudges adding intrusive and unnecessary clutter? Too few words leave readers hungry for clarity. Too many give them indigestion. As long as the sequence of events can be understood by the reader, consider refining.

Problematic told prose

In the first three examples of the four below, I've butchered some beautifully rendered shown prose to demonstrate how a told timeline can be problematic.

> I took a deep breath before walking into the kitchen.
>
> Parren was lighting a cigar from one of the candles on the table. After leaning back with a smile, he blew smoke into the air.
>
> ... the helicopter settled onto the wet sand of the beach. Uniformed men jumped out before flinging open the big side door.
>
> When the lights turned red, she slammed on the brakes.

In the first excerpt, *before* pulls us away from the moment of the deep breath, and in doing so destroys the tension. In the second excerpt, *after* shoves us past the leaning back and smiling before we've had a chance to savour the movement; it's already gone, even though we're still reading about it. In the third excerpt, *before* saps the suspense from the final sentence. We're focused on the told timeline rather than the action. And in the final example, *when* draws our attention away from the immediacy of the slammed brakes and onto the moment in time that the lights are changing.

The fix

Here are the original shown versions of the three published excerpts, and my recast of the fourth example. Notice how we know the order in which the events take place because we're shown by the very structure of the sentences.

> I took a deep breath and walked into the kitchen. (*The Chalk Man*, C. J. Tudor, p. 92)
>
> Parren was lighting a cigar from one of the candles on the table. He leaned back with a smile and blew smoke into

> the air. (*The Dream Archipelago*, Christopher Priest, p. 201)

> ... the helicopter settled onto the wet sand of the beach. Uniformed men jumped out and flung open the big side door. (*Jurassic Park*, Michael Crichton, Prologue from Kindle edition)

> The lights turned red and she slammed on the brakes.

In the Tudor excerpt, the *and* between the initial breath and the walk into the kitchen is a fine example of the power of a conjunction. It's almost invisible, which gives us the space to take that breath with the viewpoint character. And having taken it, we're ready to go into the kitchen with them.

With the Priest example, now it's as if we're in the room, watching the man as he smiles and leans back. There's space for that action to have its moment. Then he blows the smoke – that's the new moment; we've left the other behind.

In Crichton excerpt, we're now shown the action. Now we can hear the chunter of the helicopter blades in the air. Who's in this helicopter? Men in uniform. They jump out. What will happen next? We're shown: they fling open the door. There's a sense of clandestine and militaristic precision to the order of play and yet no obvious nudges as to what happens when.

And in the final example, when the brake-slamming takes place is obvious. Being told when it happens would distract us from the immediacy of the driver's response.

Shown prose that works

Take a look at this excerpt from *The Devil's Dice* by Roz Watkins (p. 79):

> I shuddered, put the laptop down and manoeuvred Hamlet onto my knee. I leant and breathed in his subtle, nutty cat smell.

Watkins doesn't tell us explicitly that the shuddering occurred before the laptop was put down, or that the laptop was moved before the character shifted the cat onto her knee. And yet we know. The sequence of events is shown by the order in which she places each clause.

- First thing that happens: shudders
- Next thing that happens: moves laptop

- Next thing that happens: manoeuvres cat
- Next thing that happens: leans
- Next thing that happens: inhales cat odour

Told prose that works

Sometimes a purposeful timeline nudge works wonders. As always in fiction, context is everything. Here's a smashing example from Chapter 41 of Will Carver's *Nothing Important Happened Today* (p. 83).

> Twelve minutes after the Lovers' brains have been completely started of oxygen, this happens:
> Two Thames River Police boats haul up on the water beneath the nine bodies. [...]
> Officers stare upwards at the ghostly mannequins swaying in the wind.
> They call them *jumpers*.
> [...] Two detectives stand between the strings of that nefarious, giant harp created by nine ropes attached to the bridge's suspension cables.
> They call them *fucking idiots*.
> The media are here. National news with the cameras pointing at the spectacle [...]
> They call them *victims*.

The *after* does indeed tap us on the shoulder and tell us about the timeline, but Carver wants us to appreciate that only *twelve minutes after* nine people have hanged themselves simultaneously, the scene is swarming with anyone and everyone who has an opinion. The viewpoint is omniscient, and the told nature of that introductory sentence sets up a cold, distant sense of reportage that's entirely appropriate. We're not supposed to be immersed in a single viewpoint or experience; the author wants us to take a cynical step back.

Summing up

Strong line craft allows readers to immerse themselves in the chronology of action by showing them, clause by clause, what's transpiring, instead of tapping them on the shoulder and telling them. If timeline nudges are telling rather than showing, recast gently and reread out loud. Is the order of play still clear? Is the prose more immersive? If so, there'll be fewer words but what's there will be all the richer.

A shown chronology is also often more suspenseful and immediate when a single character viewpoint is in play. However, think about what's possible with an omniscient narrative, and take care to respect the powerful, even disparaging distance that a told chronology might offer.

12. Emotionally evocative scenes

Clues to potential problems
Here's what to watch out for: weak verbs, repetition, purple prose.

Overview
Writing evocative scenes doesn't mean nothing can be told; after all, telling is literally one half of storytelling. 'Show, don't tell' is about choosing *what* to tell so that another thing – something important, something that will deepen our connection with a character or our understanding of the story – is shown. The line between showing and telling is therefore blurred.

We're told that a man grimaces and grabs his bloody arm; that shows us he's in pain. We're told that a boy jumps when his name is called; that shows us he's been taken by surprise. We're told that ground is carpeted with rust-coloured leaves; that shows us it's autumn. We're told that a man rubs the scar on his aching leg; that shows us he's been hurt in the past. Or perhaps we're just told something that shows us nothing but the door that leads to our own imagination.

What to consider

- Showing needn't mean reams of sensory description; it can take the form of one strong verb – a *how* verb. A woman's walking is told prose; her limping is shown prose – the how of her walking. A girl's speaking is told prose; her gabbling is shown prose – the how of her speaking. Or emotion might be evoked by a powerful adjective: A bright light tells of intensity; a blinding light shows us the impact of that intensity.

- Will telling flatten the prose or get the job done? Will showing clutter the prose or deepen engagement?

- If you decide to show, watch out for telling what you've shown. The reader only needs to know once! Doubling down with an extra tap on the shoulder tells them one of two things; either you don't trust them to understand your words or you lack confidence in your writing.

- Consider the narration style: Omniscient perspectives can feel distant, but when they're done well, that distance can be used for good intent – to bypass the weight of individual characters' emotions and allow the reader to do all the work. And first-person narratives are ones in which we're already in the character's head. Too much showing of emotion might seem contrived. Tight told prose allows the reader to decorate the story with their own imagination.
- Think about pace too. Shown prose that delves deeper into emotions can moderate the pacing. If that's interruptive, straight telling could be the order of the day.

Problematic told prose

This scene is from the first novel written by a beginner writer who kindly agreed to let me use it as a teaching tool. A commander is prepping for an attack and the atmosphere is supposed to be tense, the reader on the edge of their seat. Instead, the prose is expository – two sentences that tell with too many words.

> Half an hour had passed and images from the drone were now starting to appear on the large television monitors in the war room. He needed the SAS men to formulate a plan of attack.

The fix

Here's how I fixed it.

> Thirty minutes later, data from the drone streamed into the war room. It was time to brief the SAS.

Now the tension is shown. I've swapped the cluttering *starting to appear* for a stronger verb that complements the data – *streamed* – which shows the movement of the data more sympathetically. And the commander's emotional state – precision under pressure – is shown through the verb *to brief* rather than the expository and wordier *to formulate a plan*.

Shown prose that works

Here's a superb example of an evocative shown scene from Blake Crouch's *Recursion*, pp. 304–5). Helena and Barry are hurtling toward a laboratory. If they don't get there in time, multiple inbound ballistic missiles will kill millions.

> [...] through her window, he glimpses the brightest light he has ever seen—an incandescent flower blooming on the eastern horizon near the cluster of downtown skyscrapers, so intense it burns his corneas as it overtakes the world.
>
> Helena's face becomes radiant, and everything in his field of vision, even the sky, is robbed of color, blanching into a brilliant, searing white.
>
> He's blind for five seconds, and when he can see again, everything happens at once.
>
> All the glass in the Jeep exploding—
>
> The pine trees in a park straight ahead bending so far sideways their tips touch the ground—
>
> Structural debris from a disintegrated strip mall streaming across the road, blown by a furious wind—
>
> A man pushing a shopping cart on the sidewalk flung fifty feet through the air—
>
> And then their Jeep is flipping, the scrape of metal against pavement deafening as the shockwave blows them across the road, sparks flying into Barry's face.
>
> As the Jeep comes to rest against the curb, the noise of the blast arrives, and it is the loudest thing he has ever heard—world-ending loud, chest-crushing loud—and a single thought rips through his mind: the detonation sound wave reached them too quickly.

In this scene, a missile has found its target and delivered its payload. Not that the author tells us this. Instead, we are *shown* what must surely have happened: First through Barry's visual experience: the light (*incandescent*, *brilliant*, *searing*); the bending pine trees; the *streaming* debris; the man in the air. And then through his aural experience: the scrape of metal; the world-ending-chest-crushingly loud blast.

Look, too, at the choice of verbs – *robbed*, *blanching*, *flung*, *rips*. They're strong so that the reader never doubts the all-consuming devastation. Rather, we ache with the knowledge of it, so visceral is the showing.

And so, with a nod to Chekhov, Crouch doesn't tell us that that moon is shining. Instead, we are shown the glint of light on broken glass, albeit in the most horrifying fashion.

Told prose that works

In David Rosenfelt's *Dead Centre* (p. 215), the viewpoint character is defending a suspect in a double-homicide case. He's just entered a room and found a dead man. We can imagine how such a vision would make us feel: shocked, upset, nauseous, frightened even. What isn't clear from the excerpt, but which is critical to why the telling works, is that this is a first-person narrative.

> There is a skylight in the bathroom, with a metal latch. One end of the rope is tied to this latch, and the other end is tied to Eddie's grotesquely twisted neck as he gently swings, his feet about eighteen inches above the bathroom floor.

The author could have shown us how the viewpoint character feels via his physical response to the discovery of the hanged man. Perhaps his knees buckle, or he trips in the doorway as he backs out, or he forgets to breathe, which causes his head to swim. All those beats would show the emotional response. Rosenfelt decides it's obvious; and other than the nudge from *grotesquely*, we're told only what can be observed, leaving us to fill in the sensory gaps.

The next example illustrates how an emotionally rich shown scene might be interruptive. Your viewpoint character is in a cafe, about to slip an important plot-centric note into another character's pocket, and the smell of coffee is making him feel sick. Now, you could show it:

> I hold my hand over my mouth, masking a dry retch as the aroma of the ground coffee beans catches in the back of my throat. The nausea subsides and I focus on the note and getting it in to Chris's pocket without anyone seeing. It's my only chance.

Or you could decide that showing would be a distraction and opt for telling it straight.

> The smell of coffee makes me want to puke but I focus on the note and getting it into Chris's pocket without anyone seeing. It's my only chance.

Summing up

Scenes can be shown or told. What matters is that the prose is tight and consists of only the words it requires. Readers' imaginations are powerful, and so the emotion in scenes can be shown with something as simple as rich, perfectly placed verbs and adjectives.

13. Reading between the lines: Is the telling showing us something?

Clues to potential problems
Here's what to watch out for: generalized information dumps that read like shopping lists.

Overview
Like character information dumps, descriptions of scenes that read like items on a menu or shopping list can render prose flat and mundane. Enriching with words and phrases that nudge the reader to imagine more than is actually told can bring an environment to life.

Context is important, however. If a character's hurtling down an alleyway during an escape, they're unlikely to notice the damp on the concrete render, the rust creeping over the pipework, or the way the sun catches the broken glass strewn over the ground. That's when short, sharp telling works best.

However, if the character's appreciation of the surroundings is the point of the scene, consider introducing shown prompts to enrich it.

What to consider

- Offer specifics rather than generalizations. For example, a bowl of fruit tells us what can be seen; a bowl of rotten fruit hints also at smells, texture, neglect.

- Show how the environment impacts on the objects that come into contact with it. For example, we might be told that there's a blizzard; or we could be shown it via the ways it blurs the view through a windscreen.

- Consider how a viewpoint character's memories are evoked by the physical environment. A faded green sofa tells us about the seating in a lounge; a faded green sofa that evokes the memory of a card game with Grandfather shows us the character's family history and their nostalgic mood.

- Focus on how the viewpoint character experiences the environment. For example, that it's been raining hard tells us what the weather is like; that the child's clothes are sodden, and heavy when they remove them, shows us how hard the rain is.

- Metaphorical movement can be used to show readers information without telling them. For example, we could be told that there's a bowl of fruit on the table that's infested with insects; however, a writhing bowl of fruit shows us the infestation.

- Still, don't forget that told prose can sometimes be layered. Beneath the shopping list there could lie texture that shows something deeper.

Problematic told prose

Imagine if Khaled Hosseini had written this in the *The Kite Runner*. This butchered version is a list that tells us what's where. If a character was sprinting though this environment, the telling would work. But that's not the purpose of this scene and so it leaves the reader wanting.

> The curved wall led into the dining room, at the centre of which was a mahogany table. On the other end was a tall marble fireplace. A large sliding glass door opened into a semi-circular terrace that overlooked two acres of backyard and rows of cherry trees. A small vegetable garden ran along the eastern wall with tomatoes, mint, peppers, and a row of corn.

The fix

In the true version below (p. 5), Hosseini brings the environment to life by *showing* us the viewpoint character's memories of how he and his family and friends interacted with it, lived their lives in it – how it was to be in that place.

This is telling infused with showing, and a lovely example of how to weave the two into narrative.

> The curved wall led into the dining room, at the centre of which was a mahogany table that could easily sit thirty guests—and, given my father's taste for extravagant parties, it did just that almost every week. On the other end of the dining room was a tall marble fireplace, always lit by the orange glow of a fire in the wintertime.

> A large sliding glass door opened into a semicircular terrace that overlooked two acres of backyard and rows of cherry trees. Baba and Ali had planted a small vegetable garden along the eastern wall: tomatoes, mint, peppers, and a row of corn that never really took. Hassan and I used to call it "the Wall of Ailing Corn."

Shown prose that works

Here are two contrasting descriptions of gardens that show the reader what the spaces look like and the economic circumstances of the owners.

The first excerpt from *The Great Gatsby* (p. 6) infuses the scene with evocative detail that puts the reader at the heart of the physical environment.

Notice how at no point does F. Scott Fitzgerald tell us that the lawn is huge or that there is this or that object in it. Instead, the space takes on a life of its own such that we discover the sundial, walls and gardens through the lawn's running, jumping and drifting over them. The reader cannot help but experience the movement of the narrator's gaze, and hence the scale and sumptuousness. But there is more – the people who own this space are surely wealthy and prosperous, though we are never told this is so.

> The lawn started at the beach and ran towards the front door for a quarter of a mile, jumping over sundials and brick walks and burning gardens – finally when it reached the house drifting up the side in bright vines as though from the momentum of its run.

The second excerpt is from *The Van* (p. 2). Roddy Doyle grounds his description of the environment in his viewpoint character's experience. We learn what kind of state the garden's in not via a told list of what's in front of the character's eyes, but via the character's experience – the decisions he's made, the work he'd done earlier in the year, the way others might perceive him.

This environment couldn't be further from the lush expanse of *The Great Gatsby*'s. It is enclosed, modest, urban. And while we cannot yet know what the owner's socioeconomic situation is, hints of impoverishment are shown through this description.

> He was tempted to have a bash at the garden but the grass was nearly all gone, he'd been cutting it so often. He'd have looked like a right gobshite bringing the lawn-

mower for a walk around a baldy garden, in the middle of November. There were weeds in under the hedge, but they could stay there. Anyway, he liked them; they made the garden look more natural. He'd painted the gate and the railings a few months back; red, and a bit of white, the Liverpool colours, but Darren didn't seem to care about that sort of thing any more.

Told prose that works

The following excerpt from Lee Child's *Killing Floor* (p. 503) illustrates how, sometimes, just telling the environment straight is the best way to keep the tension high and the pace on point. Jack Reacher is staking out a warehouse. We're in the moment with him as, gun cocked, head low, he sneaks in and tells us what he sees.

> There were a hundred arc lights bolted up inside the roof of the warehouse. They lit the place up brighter than day. It was a big space. Must have been a hundred feet long, maybe eighty deep. Maybe sixty feet high. And it was full of dollar bills. A gigantic dune of money filled the whole shed. It was piled maybe fifty feet high into the back far corner.

This is reportage, and it works precisely because of this. Reacher's focus isn't on the detail; he doesn't have that luxury. Such luxury would indicate a loss in concentration, could even get him killed. And so readers are given the nuts and bolts of what can be observed in those precious seconds, and the scene is all the more immersive for it.

Told prose can be layered, too, such that shown meaning lies just beneath the surface of the shopping list. There are oodles of examples in Bret Easton Ellis's *American Psycho*. The excerpt below is taken from pp. 104–5.

> Reed Thompson walks in wearing a wool plaid four-button double-breasted suit and a striped cotton shirt and a silk tie, all Armani, plus slightly tacky blue cotton socks by Interwoven and Ferragamo cap-toe shoes that look exactly like mine, with a copy of the *Wall Street Journal* held in a nicely manicured fist and a Bill Kaiserman tweed balmacaan overcoat draped casually across the other arm. He nods and sits across from us at the table. Soon after, Todd Broderick walks in wearing a wool chalk-striped, double-breasted suit and a striped broadcloth shirt and silk

tie, all by Polo, plus an affected linen pocket square that I'm fairly sure is also by Polo. McDermott walks in next, carrying a copy of this week's *New York* magazine and this morning's *Financial Times*, wearing new nonprescription Oliver Peoples redwood-framed glasses, black and white wool houndstooth-check single-breasted suit with notch lapels, a striped cotton dress shirt with spread collar and a silk paisley tie, all of it designed and tailored by John Reyle.

The exposition here is powerful precisely because it's not really about the shopping list of stuff at all; it's about Patrick Bateman's obsessive materialism and narcissism. That, not what everyone's wearing, is what we're being shown.

And if we're bored by his long lists then all well and good. We're supposed to be. He's supposed to bore us, annoy us, repel us, frustrate us, and later frighten us. Consider voice too. Bateman lacks empathy. The flat, told prose reflects this.

He makes for a tricky protagonist because we don't want to invest in him or his success. Instead, the author gives us a backdoor – a way to invest *in our antagonism* towards him. And in doing so we come closer to glimpsing his pathology.

Summing up

Environments can be enriched with metaphor, movement, memory, and strong verbs that nudge the reader towards imagining more than has been told. Only a word or two might do the trick; if there's space for deeper contemplation, a writer might indulge in a few sentences. However, if the narrative distance is close, and the tension high, a straight tell could well be the best option for retaining immediacy.

Think, too, about what the told prose is really doing. If it's truly an info dump about *stuff* and offered only so that we know what's in that environment, a rethink might be in order. If, however, reading between the lines of that exposition reveals something far more interesting – a hidden show – then there's magic in play!

14. The non-viewpoint character's world

Clues to potential problems
Here's what to watch out for: Non-viewpoint character thoughts and emotions in first- and third-person narrations.

Overview
Point of view (POV or viewpoint) describes whose head we're in when we read a book – from whose perspective we discover what's going on – and the smells, sounds, sights and emotions involved.

When the narration style is **first person** and **third-person limited or objective**, readers are limited to a single character's experience – what they see, hear, feel and think.

When the narration style is **third-person omniscient**, the narrator (and therefore the reader) knows everything, more than an observer or any of the individual characters – backstory, motivations, intentions, emotions – and in the past, present, and future. However, it comes with limitations.

> The removed voice of the narrator, and their omniscient knowledge, makes it difficult for readers to invest emotionally in the focus characters because we're not truly experiencing what they're experiencing. It's always filtered through the all-knowing narrator, who possesses knowledge they don't. (*Making Sense of Point of View*, p. 22)

Contemporary fiction writers tend to favour first- and third-person limited. Having a single viewpoint character within a chapter or section shortens the narrative distance and allows the reader to experience the story as if they are in it.

Problems can arise when the writer wants the reader to understand how a non-POV character is feeling or what they're thinking. Instead of showing us what can be observed or heard, they tell us what those characters' motivations, thoughts and emotions are.

When that happens, we say they've dropped viewpoint, or failed to hold viewpoint, or have head-hopped.

What to consider

- Who is the POV character? Once you know this, you know what you can *tell*: thoughts, motivations, emotions, and the five senses – sight, smell, hearing, touch and taste.

- Non-POV characters' thoughts, motivations and emotions must be *shown* through audible and observable behaviour. For example, readers can be told that the butter tasted rancid on the POV character's tongue, but if a non-POV character eats the rancid butter, we must be shown their response; perhaps they gag or spit out the butter.

- Since readers have access to audible behaviour, non-POV characters can tell their own emotions, thoughts and motivations via dialogue.

- What's the narration style? Third person is the most flexible of viewpoints, but also the one where head-hopping is most likely to occur. First person is more restrictive, but the reader's less likely to notice slips because they're so grounded in the narrator's interior experience.

Problematic told prose

The example below is borrowed from an independent author I've worked with. I've masked their prose to protect their intellectual property, retaining the essence of the problem.

Emily is the mother. Charlotte is the viewpoint character; we experience the world through her. The narration style is third-person limited. Or at least it should be. In the excerpt below, we shift from Charlotte's experience into an omniscient viewpoint whereby we are told the external experience of three people ('resisted the urge to giggle').

> George produced his antique gold pocket watch – a mere affectation given that the clock on the mantle had never lost a beat. Emily and her daughters duly resisted the urge to giggle.

The fix

In this edited version, I've shown Emily's resistance with her movement, and changed the told element so that it's rooted firmly in Charlotte's experience.

> George produced his antique gold pocket watch – a mere affectation given that the clock on the mantle had never lost a beat. Her mother put her hand on her mouth and dipped her chin. Charlotte resisted the urge to giggle.

Shown prose that works

In this example from *Girl with a Pearl Earring* (p. 175), Frans has been assigned difficult work at a kiln and is struggling. He's a non-POV character so he could tell us via the dialogue that he's struggling, but he's trying to put on a brave face in front of his sister, the POV character. The author shows us his struggle via the back door of what his sister can observe.

> Frans pulled the cloths from his arms, wiped his face with a rag and gulped beer from a mug. He leaned against the wall and rolled his shoulders the way men do who have finished unloading cargo from a canal boat and are easing and stretching their muscles. I had never seen him make such a gesture before.

It's a beautiful example of shown prose that holds viewpoint but ensures we're alert to the ache in Frans's back and shoulders.

Here's a short excerpt from (*29 Seconds*, p. 332). Marie is a non-POV character so we can't access her emotional state. Instead, we're shown it – it's shame, and it's expressed by what can be observed: her posture and the direction of her gaze.

> Marie paused, her shoulders slumped. She spoke without looking up from the floor.

Told prose that works

Dialogue can be used to tell a non-POV character's thoughts and feelings. Just bear in mind that it need not be necessarily reliable. What a character says and what they think are two different things. Being able to access voice *and* motivation is what often makes viewpoint characters interesting. With non-POV characters we only have half the story. That's why showing observable and audible behaviour is often more effective.

Still, there's nothing wrong with a non-POV character expressing their emotions through speech. It can be more interesting to be shown their movements, but if that's creating clutter, a straight vocal tell will be just the ticket, as long as it's rich in purpose.

Bear in mind too that with deep narration styles, **assumptive telling** of a non-POV character's emotional experience might well work. By this, I mean that the narrative has a spoken feel to it, one in which the viewpoint character's *perceptions* are embedded. In this excerpt from *The Cold Cold Ground* (p. 260), the 'she' (Laura) is *not* the viewpoint character.

> I had no appetite. I told her about my ride with Billy.
> She was horrified. "How can they just lift you off the street like that? The nerve of them!"
> I told her about my pet theory.

Notice that we're given Laura's internal experience (*was horrified*), which could – strictly speaking – be seen as a telling of emotion that we shouldn't have access to. And yet it doesn't jar. There are two reasons for this.

- First, author Adrian McKinty has chosen a tight first-person narration style for this book – I did this, I said that. And so when we read 'She was horrified' it's actually just shorthand for the viewpoint character's assumption. He might as well have have said, 'She seemed horrified' or 'She looked horrified'. First-person narrations ground us so deeply in a POV character's head that subtle shifts don't always knock us off balance and feel like head-hopping.

- Second, the dialogue that follows this little telling *shows* her emotion, and that's where we're focused. Even a pedant would be hard-pressed not to move forward.

Summing up

Consider what the POV character already knows, what they can observe or hear in relation to a non-POV character, and what they can infer from that information. That will determine what they can report. What they report allows readers to access the internal experience of the non-viewpoint character through a back door.

Take note of the narration style too, though. If you're writing in a deep, limited narration style, particularly first person, little told nudges – ones that are shorthand assumptions – could well keep the pace on point and the story moving forward without pulling readers out of the POV character's gaze.

15. In and around dialogue

Clues to potential problems
Here's what to watch out for: maid-and-butler dialogue; unnecessary tags that repeat punctuation; tags that repeat voice, mood and intention; phrases such as *in a voice of*, *in a tone of*.

Overview
Great dialogue shows us the speaker's voice, mood and intention. Great dialogue tags show us who's speaking. Great action beats show the physicality of the speaker and are superb backdoors to non-viewpoint characters' emotionality. And free indirect style can show a viewpoint character's interiority when the dialogue needs to focus elsewhere and where a direct thought would seem contrived.

What to consider

- Is the dialogue being used as a platform for backstory exposition? If so, maid-and-butler speech could be in play.

- Do speech tags tell what the dialogue's punctuation already shows?

- Do speech tags tell what the words in the dialogue already show?

- Might action beats do a better job of showing a non-viewpoint character's mood if the dialogue feels too told?

- And perhaps free indirect style might show a viewpoint character's state of mind more effectively than a told direct thought if the narration style is third person.

- Consider, too, the narration style. First person narratives are so deeply grounded in the character's interior space that even told prose needn't feel like flat exposition but a more personal disclosure.

- And don't forget the narrative pace and genre register. Exposition in a high-octane thriller can interrupt dialogue and narrative. In a crime novel that's steeped in historical detail, a fantasy or an off-world space opera, the pace might be gentler, the register non-contemporary. Telling can dislocate the prose from the here and now, and lend it an otherworldly/othertimely feel.

Problematic told prose: Maid-and-butler dialogue

When Character X tells Character Y something that Y already knows just so the reader can access need-to-know information, maid-and-butler dialogue is in play.

Here's an example of what it looks like, courtesy of a beginner author who kindly gave me permission to use it for teaching material.

> Thacker flew to London. That's where he'd focus his search. But he'd need help. From his hotel in Bond Street, he called Lindy Lund, his chief operating officer.
>
> 'Hello, Lindy. I am in London and will be staying here for maybe a week or two. Couple of things you could do for me. First, could you send over two of our best operatives? The business in London may get ugly. I will need armed men.'
>
> 'Can you tell me about your assignment?'
>
> Thacker replied, 'For the moment, no. The second request is less precise. About two years ago, we had a contract with a South African mining company to provide them security for their diamonds in transit between different locations. There was a heist. The gang got away with the haul, but they were soon captured. During the interrogation of the gang leaders, it transpired that they had planned to smuggle the diamonds to the UK where they would be fenced in London. The police managed to extract a good deal of information about the London gang engaged in smuggling diamonds. I need to know all you can find out. In particular the name of the London gang leader and how large their network is.'
>
> Lund said, 'Yes, I remember the incident well. We didn't cover ourselves with glory. We lost two of our men in the gunfight. The result was loss of a lucrative contract, and having to pay hefty compensation to the widows and families of the two dead men. I'll search our records and files. We have good contacts with the South African police. I am sure they will let us have access to their records too. How long have I got?'

Notice how Lund remembers the incident well, which puts the necessity of it being told through dialogue into doubt. And Thacker has read all the files, meaning he should know the outcome of the op; Lund's telling him through dialogue makes no sense. And yet the reader needs to know this information. One solution is to recast the summary as narrative.

The fix

This is how I edited it. It's still told prose – information without sensory experience – but it's been consolidated outside the dialogue and is obviously for the reader.

> Thacker flew to London. That's where he'd focus his search. But he'd need help. From his hotel in Bond Street, he called Lindy Lund, his chief operating officer.
>
> 'I need you to do two things for me. First, send over two of our best operatives. The business in London might get ugly. I'll need armed men.'
>
> 'Can you tell me about the assignment?'
>
> 'For the moment, no. The second request requires a little more leg work. Remember the heist a couple of years ago?'
>
> They'd provided a South African diamond-mining company with security during transit of their stones. However, they'd been compromised. The gang responsible got away with the haul. They were soon captured, though not before two of Thacker's men had been killed in the gunfight. They'd lost a lucrative contract and been stung with a hefty compensation pay-out to the widows.
>
> 'The police extracted a good deal of information and I need it, particularly anything on the organisation assigned to handle the fencing in London and how large their network is.'
>
> Lund said, 'Yes, I remember the incident well. We didn't cover ourselves with glory. I'll search our records and speak to the South African police. How long have I got?'

Problematic told prose: Dialogue tags

Dialogue tags – or speech tags – are what writers use to indicate which character is speaking. Their function is, for the most part, mechanical. Problems include the following:

- The tag tells the mood already shown through the dialogue
- The tag tells what's already been shown by punctuation

The examples below illustrate the problems.

> 'Oh, come on. You don't really believe that, do you?' Ralph said **sceptically**.
>
> 'Ralph! Come inside. That's an order,' Jane **demanded**.
>
> "I read some of your stuff online," the professor said. "Much of it is crudely put but you're probably the only person who dares to express what's being left unsaid. That's why I—"
>
> "Really?" Marcus **interrupted him**. "And what's being left unsaid?"
>
> 'Omar!' Marnie **exclaimed**, and rushed over to him.

The fix

In the first example, the adverb tells of the scepticism already shown by the speech. We can remove it safely and let the dialogue stand on its own two feet.

> 'Oh, come on. You don't really believe that, do you?'
> Ralph said.

In the second example, the verb *demanded* tells what's already been shown by the dialogue. Again, we can replace it with a less showy tag ('said') that doesn't distract. If it's clear that Jane is speaking, we could remove the tag altogether or replace it with an action beat that shows her mood.

> 'Ralph! Come inside. That's an order,' Jane said.
>
> 'Ralph! Come inside. That's an order.'
>
> Jane slammed the baton against the table. 'Ralph! Come inside. That's an order.'

In the third example, the em dash before the closing quote marks is a conventional way of showing that speech has been interrupted. 'Marcus interrupted him' is therefore an unnecessary tell. We can replace with a more straightforward tag that allows the punctuation to take centre stage.

> "I read some of your stuff online," the professor said. "Much of it is crudely put but you're probably the only person who dares to express what's being left unsaid. That's why I—"
>
> "Really?" Marcus said. "And what's being left unsaid?"

And in the fourth example, the exclamation mark shows the exclamation and is therefore redundant in the tag. Removing it and turning the tag into an action beat is one solution.

> 'Omar!' Marnie rushed over to him.

Problematic told prose: Filtering in thoughts

Thoughts are a valuable way of allowing us access to a character's deepest emotions and perceptions. They're more immediate than even a deep third-person narration style and therefore useful when the author wants to narrow the psychic distance between reader and viewpoint character.

Problems arise when there's an abundance of told thinking going on. It's a form of filtering (see Chapter 3) and overuse can be interruptive. Here are three examples, courtesy of a generous client who gave me permission to use their unedited drafts for teaching purposes.

> Twill lets himself be led by the elbow and eases himself into the chair opposite, **thinking to himself** how few people in the world could get away with this. Perhaps only the one.
>
> He's either extremely confused or an exceptional actor. Twill **has already decided** he's no actor.
>
> Twill hasn't met any of Cromer's family but a toothy young man in army fatigues stands out. **He thinks** that has to be his son.

The fix

One solution is to employ free indirect speech (sometimes called free indirect discourse or free indirect speech). This offers the essence of first-person thought but through a third-person viewpoint. FIS keeps the character's voice foremost but omits the clutter of speech marks, speech tags and italic. Normal body-text style is used because FIS uses the same base tense and narrator as the main narrative.

I think there's a rather delicious certainty to the second telling ('has already decided') and wouldn't necessarily want to edit it. However, the unfiltered versions, edited using FIS, might looks as follows:

> Twill lets himself be led by the elbow and eases himself into the chair opposite. Few people in the world could get away with this. Perhaps only the one.
>
> He's either extremely confused or an exceptional actor. No, the man's no actor.
>
> Twill hasn't met any of Cromer's family, but a toothy young man in army fatigues stands out. Has to be his son.

Shown prose that works

Here's an example from the same client, this time demonstrating their mastery of *showing* backstory through a combination of dialogue and narrative. This author doesn't fall into the trap of having his two characters discuss what they both already know. Instead, one guy probes, while Twill (the viewpoint character) is reticent, as shown by the shortness of his answers. The emotional voices are strong and nudge the reader towards understanding – Twill is hurting on the inside and the outside. And then it's through narrative that we're given information that begins to unveil the past.

> 'You all settled in at your ma's?'
> 'S'okay.'
> 'Gonna stay there?'
> Twill blinks. 'Maybe. Lots of memories.'
> 'How long's it been?'
> 'Couple of years. They knock me out. I s'pose it stops me thinking about my leg.'
> 'Is that a bad thing?'
> Twill thinks back to a wood in Belgium and a young man in sportswear with his head twisted at an impossible angle. 'It has its ... downsides.'

Questions, arguments, confusion and compassion within speech all help writers turn told information into shown emotional revelation.

Told prose that works

The Thacker/Lund example earlier illustrated how a told narrative can drive story forward. Cluttering with sensory information in that case would have interrupted the dialogue. It's a good reminder that there's no room for 'don't tell' when it comes to writing and editing fiction. As with most things, it depends on context and what's required in the moment.

Narrative pace and setting should be considered too. Here are some examples from C.J. Sansom's *Tombland* (pp. 150–51). The book is set a couple of years after the death of Henry VIII. An abundance of told beats report on non-viewpoint characters' expressions and voice tones. Sansom could have opted for shown speech tags – stronger verbs like *spat*, *shouted*, *barked* or *hissed* instead of the adverbs and adverbial phrases that tell of voice: *in a voice of, in a tone of*.

> He said, **his voice angry from the start**, 'My wife, Jane, and my servant, Goodman Michael Vowell. They can stay there, we will not be long.'
>
> 'My daughter is dead and gone.' She spoke **in a voice of utter weariness**. 'In a few days her husband will be tried. What is there to investigate?'
>
> 'But it is too late, Master Hunchback Sergeant, John Boleyn is guilty, and in a few days will be dangling from the Norwich gallows.' **He spoke this last sentence with satisfaction**.
>
> 'We have been asked only to review the matter,' **I answered quietly**. Will you be giving evidence, sir?'
>
> 'I do not know,' Reynolds said, **in a tone of quiet, fierce anger**. 'I can hardly bear even to go out, to see all the nosy glances. As for my hopes of the mayoralty next year, those are finished.'
>
> I thought, Was that all his daughter's death meant to him, but **Nicholas said sympathetically**. 'What happened must have been a great shock to you, sir.'
>
> 'A great shock?' **Reynolds's voice rose in anger**. 'Nine years ago my ...'

In a contemporary mystery, such as a Harlan Coben novel, the prose might read as flat and disjointed, but not in this historical setting. The voice/tone is told, the register slightly formal. Yet it feels deliberate, as if the intention is to force the reader to acknowledge that they're spying on the past rather than the now. And yet there's an intimacy in the first-person narration, too – one that grounds the telling in opinion rather than reportage. It's telling with substance.

Summing up

Dialogue with the right words and appropriate punctuation can show plenty. The key is to ensure that what's revealed isn't told again via tags and action beats that add nothing new.

It also needs to show a story unveiling, and in a manner that's authentic. Characters have to earn their speech. When their words are offered for no other purpose than to fill in gaps for the reader, there's a problem, though the solution needn't necessarily be a shown one. It could be a short piece of told narrative that's snappy enough to clue us in without interrupting the characters' chitchat.

16. A box of showing tools

Overview
This final chapter reviews a selection of literary devices that writers and editors can use to draw the reader deeper into a character's interior space.

Action beats
Action beats are short descriptions that come before, between or just after dialogue. In addition to grounding dialogue within a physical environment, they are a backdoor to showing non-viewpoint-character emotions via observable and audible behaviour.

Use with care in third-person-limited and first-person narrations because the reader is seeing the world through the viewpoint character's eyes. A blushing POV character will feel the heat on their cheeks but won't be able to report that their face is bright red unless they have access to a mirror.

Examples

- **Shows a non-POV character's anxiety (*The Good Daughter*, p. 385):**

    "I didn't believe he would die." Charlie grabbed her hair in her hands. "I mean, I knew it would happen, but I didn't think it would. Like, the opposite of when you buy a lottery ticket."

- **Shows a non-POV character's dismissiveness (*Tombland*, p. 42):**

    'Oh tush,' she said, waving a hand. 'I have known many hunchbacks who have married, and far worse-looking that you.'

Alliteration
Alliteration is the repetition of sounds at the beginning of words in quick succession. The result is a playful, musical rhythm that can infuse prose with merriment (even when the subject matter is dark), excitement, and urgency. Experiment with softer consonants to show calmness; employ

harder ones to evoke spite and bitterness. Overall, alliteration is an attention-grabbing tool for authors who want to show rather than tell mood.

Examples

- **Shows the narrator's upbeat mood (*Cooking for Cannibals*, p. 18):**

   It was a modern marvel of medicinal manufacturing. Sikorski's drug would change the course of human history if and when it was approved by the cogs in the arcane machinery of the U.S. Food & Drug Administration.

- **Shows the frenzied nature of the feasting (*Cooking for Cannibals*, p. 399):**

   Lunch was more man meat. Then more Olympics. Then a meat-filled, mid-afternoon feast (Brazilian empanadas). Then more Olympics. Then dinner, a masterful, multi-course, multinational menu comprising human meat and nothing but human meat.

Anaphora

Anaphora is the deliberate repetition of words or phrases at the beginning of successive clauses such that the reader is forced to emphasize them. This is a great tool for showing passion, hysteria, anger and disbelief.

Examples

- **Shows the speaker's incredulity:**

   'But surely this was before he made the decision to blackmail you, before he decided to contact your office, before he told your partner, indeed before he did anything that might put your job and your relationship in jeopardy.'

- **Shows the speaker's frustration (*The Good Daughter*, p. 43):**

   She gripped the cell phone in her hand as she turned a corner. The wrong boy. The wrong man. The wrong phone. The wrong way because she didn't know where the hell she was going.

Asyndeton

Asyndeton is a rhythmic tool in which the sentence structure follows the pattern A, B, C. Note the omission of a final conjunction such as *and* or *but*. Removing these accelerates the pace of the sentence, which is useful for authors who want to show emotions such as panic, frustration, fear, shock and confusion, and in situations where a character is acting on impulse, facing danger, or in a chase scene.

Examples

- **Shows the POV character's heightened state of alert (*Places in the Darkness*, p. 237):**

  'Freitas raises his head as she approaches, begins reaching towards her, stops himself.'

- **Shows the character's despair (*Cockroaches*, p. 477–8):**

  She wailed and cried for her shattered life, her broken dreams, the telephone call two years before, the chaplain's visit to her door, the X-rays, the filthy hospitals, the unstoppable hiss of the respirator.

Free indirect speech

Free indirect speech (sometimes called free indirect discourse or free indirect style) offers the essence of first-person thought but through a third-person viewpoint and without deviating from the novel's base tense.

Examples

- **Shows the POV character's natural voice and his realization (*Recursion*, p. 158):**

  He doesn't know what to say to her. Strike that. He knows. He had always blamed Meghan's death for his and Julia's demise. It was their family—the *three* of them—that united him and Julia.

- **Shows the POV character's natural voice and her frustration (*The Outsider*, p. 256):**

  All right, reporters had come to call, also the police, and Mrs Kelly, as the out-front person at the Heisman

Memory Unit, had had to put up with them. But their questions hadn't been about Terry Maitland, or she would have known he was dead. So what had been the great big fracking deal?

Juxtaposition

When two incongruous ideas, entities or settings are placed next to each other, their proximity can feel uncomfortable or surprising and arouse a heightened sense of shock, grief, irony or absurdity.

Example

- **Shows the character's hysteria (*The Outsider*, pp. 99–100).** The setting is the aftermath of a wake for a murdered boy. In the kitchen, his mother begins to laugh and throw food around. The scene conjures a slapstick comedy sketch, one that butts up awkwardly, obscenely even, against the reason for the event. Through the juxtaposition we are shown the woman's utter devastation:

    Arleen slipped under his hands and darted towards one of the counters, still laughing and howling. She grabbed a serving dish of lasagna in both hands – it had been brought by one of Father Brixton's sycophants – and dumped it on her head. Cold pasta fell into her hair and onto her shoulders. She heaved the dish into the living room.
    '*Frankie is dead and we've got a fucking Italian buffet!*'

One-line paragraphs

Single-line paragraphs act as pacing tools. Every time a reader moves to a new line, they take a pause. The effect is a staccato rhythm in which the reader is shown the viewpoint character's intimate experience of a series of micro dramas as they unfold moment by moment, tiny paragraph by tiny paragraph.

Examples

In these first two examples, the sentence fragments play a big part in showing immediacy, but the layout does the heavy lifting in relation to the reveal.

- **Shows immediacy – the character's experience in the moment (*Dark Matter*, both examples p. 225):**

    It becomes so quiet I can hear the escalated beating of my own heart.
    And then—something impossible.
    A sound.
    Far, far down the corridor.
    Amanda looks at me.

    I take a step back, and as they draw closer, I'm tempted to run, but where would I go?
    Might as well face it.
    It's a man.
    He's naked.
    His skin covered in mud or dirt or …
    Blood.
    Definitely blood.

- **Shows immediacy – the character's experience in the moment – despite the third-person past tense (*Cooking for Cannibals*, p. 18):**

    And while Sikorski's endless iterations of experimental white powder had increasingly produced anti-aging properties, they'd also delivered some terrible, sometimes bizarre, side effects—death, of course, being the worst.
    Until now.
    Now, the drug worked wonders.

Onomatopoeia

Onomatopoeic words sound like the noise made by the thing they're referring to. That makes them useful showing tools that help keep prose lean and evoke sensory experience. Examples include nouns such as *buzz*, *click*, *thwack*, *thump*, *boom*, *splat*, and *whoosh* and their verbed equivalents.

Examples

- **Shows the rhythm of background music (*The Chalk Man*, p. 7):**

I could already hear the faint thump, thump of the fairground music, and smell the burgers and candyfloss. Today was going to be perfect.

- **Shows sensory experience of the baton slapping against the officer's hands (*The Outsider*, p. 112):**

    Thuck-thuck-thuck.
    It was a cop, tapping with his nightstick. Patient. Now making a cranking gesture with his free hand: roll it down.
    For a moment, Merl had no idea where he was […]

- **Shows sensory experience of approaching footsteps (*Cockroaches*, p. 429):**

    The sound of vibrating metal. Clang, clang, clang. They were on their way up the ladder.

Polysyndeton

Polysyndeton is a rhythmic tool through which a sentence's structure follows the pattern A and B and C. Note the omission of commas. Depending on context, polysyndetic structures can either accelerate the pace, thereby showing dizziness, giddiness, hysteria or excitement, or decelerate it, thereby showing drudgery or banality.

It can also be a useful tool for those who want to mark the passage of a lengthy period time quickly but in a way that captures the rhythm of physical change.

Examples

- **Shows the rhythmic passage of time (*Reservoir 13*, p. 138):**

    The clocks went forward and the evenings opened up and the days stood a little straighter on their feet.

- **Shows relentless drudgery (*The Road*, p. 226):**

    There was a creek some hundred yards from the house and he hauled endless pails of water across the stubble fields and the mud and they heated water and bathed in a tub off the back bedroom on the lower floor and he cut their hair and shaved his beard.

- **Shows the viewpoint character's giddiness** (*The Girl in the Red Coat*, p. 151).

    I play tea sets with the twins on a fold-up table and their voices go very fast and gabbling like chipmunks and they lift the cups to their lips and pretend to drink, over and over, and their hands move across the table, swapping things about so fast I feel dizzy.

Punctuation and formatting

Punctuation and formatting are small but powerful tools that indicate when to start, when to stop, when to pause, which words to stress, the volume at which they would be spoken out loud. Here's a brief summary of those with a showing function that needn't be accompanied by a written tell.

- **Ellipses** show pauses within dialogue and narrative, and trailing-off speech at the end of dialogue.
- **Exclamation marks** show surprise, shock, enthusiasm and joy. They can also add an imperative tone and add volume to speech. Take care not to overuse them because too many can make a reader feel like they're being punched repeatedly.
- **Question marks** show enquiry. Restrict them to direct questions; they're not necessary at the end of sentences that begin with the likes of *Perhaps* and *Surely* or other wonderments.
- **Quotation marks** show that a character is speaking. When placed around a single word or phrase, they show scepticism. Avoid using for thoughts.
- **Italic text** shows emphasis when used with single words and short phrases. It can be used to indicate a character's direct thought.
- **Em dashes** at the end of dialogue show interruptions.
- **Capitalized text** shows volume. Restrict its use and consider action beats that might convey loudness more creatively.

For a more detailed analysis of how to use punctuation in fiction, take a look at *Making Sense of Punctuation*.

Sentence fragments

Sentence fragments purposefully omit something – sometimes a subject, sometimes a verb. The rhythm is choppy, allowing authors to show tension-related emotions such fear, alarm, panic, anxiety and jumpiness.

However, sentence fragments make for more interesting exposition, too; they remove the expletives from told lists and imbue them with a sense of the viewpoint character's discovery – a subtle and immediate reveal rather than a boring shopping list. These work well for scenes in which characters are scrutinizing, evaluating, investigating, measuring, and where the author wants to convey clinical precision.

Examples

- **Shows POV character's wariness (*Life Deluxe*, Kindle edition):**

    The Iranian hugged him. Pounded him on the back. Cut him with verbal knives.

- **Shows a sense of discovery (*Parting Shot*, p. 342):**

    Duckworth read the labels. Modems, chargers, cables. But more interesting things, too. Surveillance-type equipment. Listening devices. Microphones.

- **Shows the character's close scrutiny (*Skein Island*, p. 82):**

    The cubes had markings on them, Carvings. Intricate work. […] They looked heraldic, or maybe older. Classical in design.

Summing up

Purposefully told prose has as much right to be in a novel as its shown sister. Both can add atmosphere, both can deepen story and character, and both can be used to control the reader's gaze. These tools help authors and editors add texture to flat, mundane text, although, as I hope is clear, this showing needn't be a grand endeavour. It can come in the form of a single word, short phrase or a punctuation mark as much as from the application of a literary device.

Glossary

Action beats are short descriptions that come before, between or just after dialogue.

Adjectives are words that describes nouns.

Adverbs and **adverbial phrases** are words that describes a verb.

Anaphora is the deliberate repetition of words or phrases at the beginning of successive clauses for artistic effect.

Asyndeton is a literary device through which a sentence's structure follows the pattern A, B, C.

Cleft sentences are those in which the conventional sentence structure is shifted in order to direct the reader's focus and emphasis (e.g. 'It's you who needs to listen' versus 'You need to listen').

Dialogue is the characters' speech.

Dialogue tags, also called **speech tags**, are words that indicate which character is speaking (e.g. Jake said).

Expletives, sometimes called **syntactic** or **grammatical expletives**, are words that shift the emphasis in a sentence and therefore have a syntactic function, but in themselves contribute nothing our understanding of the sentence and therefore have no sematic role (e.g. there is/were, it is/was). You might also hear them called **empty** or **filler words**.

Exposition is the introduction of information. When poorly executed and overblown it can be boring, distracting and distancing.

Filter words are verbs that tell us how a character is accessing experience rather than showing us what they're experiencing (e.g. *noticed*, *realized*, *seemed*, *spotted*, *saw*).

Free indirect speech (sometimes called **free indirect discourse** or **free indirect style**) offers the essence of first-person thought but through a third-person viewpoint. It retains the base tense.

Head-hopping is a narrative misfire in which readers are forced to jump from one character's perspective (thoughts and experiences) to another's. It's a viewpoint problem.

Narrative distance, sometimes called **psychic distance**, describes how close the reader feels to the narrator. When a novel is being narrated by a particular character (for example, in first-person and third-person limited narrations), it will describe how connected we feel to that person and their experience.

Narrative means story. It's the part of the book that isn't dialogue.

Non-viewpoint characters are any other characters in a scene or chapter whose behaviour can be observed or heard or discussed. We don't have access to their internal experience (thoughts, emotions, knowledge, motivations, intentions, and so on).

Omniscient point of view is a narrative style in which the reader accesses the story through the eyes of a distinctive, external all-knowing narrator as opposed to a single character.

Overwriting is characterized by too many words on the page. Repetition and redundancy are often in play.

Point of view, **viewpoint** and **POV** are used interchangeably to describe whose head the reader is in when they read the story, whose perspective we experience the story through.

Polysyndeton: Literary device through which a sentence's structure follows the pattern A and B and C.

Pronouns are words that replace nouns (e.g. I, you, he, she, we, me, it, this, that, them, those, myself, who, whom).

Psychic distance: see **narrative distance**.

Purple prose is overblown, poorly structured writing with strings of extraneous and often multisyllabic adjectives and adverbs.

Quotation marks or **speech marks** indicate the spoken word. Singles or doubles are acceptable but authors and editors should enforce consistency.

Shown prose relates characters' experience through actions and sensory information.

Third-person limited refers to a narration style in which the internal experiences (thoughts, feelings, motivations etc.) of a single character – the viewpoint character – are related.

Told prose relates characters' experience through exposition (the introduction of information rather than actions and sensory information).

Verbs describe doing. They can refer to physical actions (e.g. digging), mental actions (e.g. wondering) or a state of being (e.g. is, are).

Viewpoint characters are those whose perspectives we experience as we read: what they think, feel, understand, know, see, hear, smell and do.

Word dumps or **information dumps** describe poorly executed exposition – description that lacks sensory detail. They're often a feature of overly told prose.

Cited sources

22 Dead Little Bodies, Stuart MacBride, HarperCollins, 2015

29 Seconds, T.M. Logan, Zaffre, 2018

A Tale of Two Cities, Charles Dickens, Chapman & Hall, 1868

American Psycho, Bret Easton Ellis, Picador, 2011

Cockroaches, Lee Child, Transworld, 2008

Cooking for Cannibals, Rich Leder, Laugh Riot Press, 2021

Dark Matter, Blake Crouch, Pan Macmillan, 2017

Day of the Accident, Nuala Ellwood, Penguin, 2019

Dead Centre, David Rosenfelt, Warner, 2007

Dead Lions, Mick Herron, John Murray, 2017

Dog Tags, David Rosefelt, Grand Central Publishing, 2010

Don't Let Go, Harlan Coben, Arrow Books, 2017

Empire of the Sun, J.G. Ballard, Harper Perennial, 2014

Ghostman, Roger Hobbs, Corgi, 2014

Girl with a Pearl Earring, Tracy Chevalier, HarperCollins, 2018

Insidious Intent, Val McDermid, Little, Brown, 2017

Jurassic Park, Michael Crichton, Kindle edition, Arrow, 2015

Killing Floor, Lee Child, Bantam, 2010

Let Me Lie, Clare Mackintosh, Sphere, 2018

Life Deluxe, Jens Lapidus, Pan, 2015, Kindle edition

Making Sense of Point of View, Louise Harnby, Panx Press, 2020

Making Sense of Punctuation, Louise Harnby, Panx Press, 2020

No One Home, Tim Weaver, Penguin, 2020

Nothing Important Happened Today, Will Carver, Orenda Books, 2019

Orphan X, Gregg Hurwitz, Penguin, 2016

Pain: Type, shape, and reaction nudges, Louise Harnby, harnby.co/show-pain

Paradise Lost, Book I, John Milton, Kindle Edition, Amazon Classics, 2017

Places in the Darkness, Chris Brookmyre, Orbit, 2017

Play Dead, David Rosenfelt, Grand Central Publishing, 2009

POC and Food Comparisons and Description Guide – Words for Skin Tone, Writing with Color, https://bit.ly/3unUFpt

Recursion, Blake Crouch, Pan Macmillan, 2019

She Lies in Wait, Gytha Lodge, Penguin, 2019

Skein Island, Aliya Whiteley, Titan, 2019

The Chalk Man, C.J. Tudor, Penguin, 2018

The Cold Cold Ground, Adrian McKinty, Serpent's Tail, 2012

The Devil's Dice, Roz Watkins, HQ, 2019

The Dream Archipelago, Christopher Priest, Gollancz, 2009

The Ghost Fields, Elly Griffiths, Quercus, 2016

The Girl in the Red Coat, Kate Hamer, Faber & Faber, 2015

The Godmother, Hannelore Cayre, Old Street Publishing, 2019

The Good Daughter, Karin Slaughter, HarperCollins, 2018

The Great Gatsby, F. Scott Fitzgerald, Wordsworth Classics, 1993

The Joy of Writing Sex, Elizabeth Benedict, Souvenir Press, 2002

The Kite Runner, Khaled Hosseini, Bloomsbury, 2007

The Outsider, Stephen King, Hodder, 2018

The Poison Artist, Jonathan Moore, Orion, 2014

The Poppy Factory, William Fairchild, Futura, 1987

The Road, Cormac McCarthy, Picador, 2009

The Silent Patient, Alex Michaelides, Orion, 2019

The Van, Roddy Doyle, Minerva, 1992

The Wife Between Us, Greer Hendricks and Sarah Pekkanen, Pan, 2018

To Kill a Devil, John A. Connell, Nailhead Publishing, 2020

Tombland, C.J. Sansom, Pan, 2018

Words for Skin Tone, Writing with Color, https://bit.ly/3bpg6ho

Printed in Great Britain
by Amazon